Clergy & Administrators
COMPENSATION

Fourth Edition

By Michael Chitwood
"The Authority"

Corinthians Kingdom Publishing House
Osborne Office Center, Suite 500
5746 Marlin Road
Chattanooga, TN 37411-4061
1-800-345-9117

The key to a useful salary survey is the accuracy in reporting an appropriate sampling of data.

Consistency is important in surveys and to maintain consistency in this survey, all data from last year was maintained.

Caution: It is important that the user of this material be qualified in a field of expertise so that addition or modification will be based upon participant's needs and recommendations.

This publication is designed to provide accurate and authoritative information in regard to the subject matter covered. It is sold with the understanding that the publisher is not engaged in rendering legal, accounting, or other professional service. If legal advice or other expert assistance is required, the services of a competent professional person should be sought. From a Declaration of Principles jointly adopted by a Committee of the American Bar Association and a Committee of Publishers and Associations.

Index

Index

Support for the Minister

"Pastors who do their work well should be paid well and should be highly appreciated, especially those who work hard at both preaching and teaching. Those who work deserve their pay!"
(1 Timothy 5:17 & 18, The Living Bible)

"For in the law God gave to Moses he said that you must not put a muzzle on an ox to keep it from eating when it is treading out the wheat. Do you suppose God was thinking only about oxen when he said this? Wasn't he also thinking about us? Of course he was. He said this to show us that Christian workers should be paid by those they help. They have planted good spiritual seeds in your souls, is it too much to ask, in return, that you give to those who preach to you. But shouldn't we have even greater right to them. The Lord has given orders that those who preach the Gospel should be supported by those who accept it."
(1 Corinthians 9:9-12, 14, The Living Bible)

God calls His ministers to serve; He calls upon His people to support them adequately.

Policy on Timing of Merit Increases

Following is the profile of organizations reporting on the prevailing practice of merit increases:

65%   grant increases to all eligible employees on the same fixed calendar date.

15%   grant increases to employees on the employee's anniversary date of hire.

9%   grant increases on random dates at the direction of the supervisor.

7%   grant increases on the anniversary date of each employee's last increase.

4%   grant increases according to some combination of the previous approaches.

Formal Salary Administration

47%   of the participants reported they had a formal merit review program or salary range system

Givers and Takers

1. For growing churches, and if you are not growing you won't be interested in this anyway.

2. If you are paying your people too low, you are starving your growth for lack of qualified people.

3. You may have more than enough people, but not qualified people.

4. You may not have enough people, so you are overworking your few good people, which means you are not planning for future growth.

Quality People = Growth = Proper Compensation = Building of the Kingdom

Definitions of Internal Terms

Compensation:

1. To recompense or reimburse.
2. Something given or received as payment or reparation, as for a service or loss.

Remuneration:

1. To pay an equivalent to for a service, loss or expense.

Pay:

1. To give money to in return for goods or services rendered.
2. The statue of being paid by an employer.
3. Something paid for as a purpose and expense, as a Salary or Wage.

Salary:

1. Fixed compensation paid regularly for services.

Value:

1. The monetary worth of something.
2. Relative worth, utility or importance; degree of excellence.
3. To rate or scale in usefulness, importance or general worth.
4. To consider or rate highly.

Estimate:

1. A numerical value obtained from a statistical sample and assigned to the population parameter.

Worth:

1. Equal in value to: Having possession or income equal to, deserving, substantial or significant value or merit.

Experience:

1. Direct observation of or participation in events or a basis of knowledge.
2. Practical knowledge, skills, or practice derived from direct observations of or participation in events or in a particular activity.
3. The length of such participation.

Appreciation:

1. An expression of admiration, approval, or gratitude.
2. Increase in value.

Stipend:

1. A fixed sum of money paid periodically for services or to defray expenses.

Definitions of Abbreviations

QAS	=	Qualified Adjusted Salaries
QAR	=	Qualified Adjusted Revenue
ARM-	=	Average Range Minimum
ARM+	=	Average Range Maximum
SW	=	Salaries & Wages
CSW	=	Classified Salaries & Wages
Y	=	Income
APR	=	Adjusted Percentage Rate
TAPR	=	Total Adjusted Percentage Rate
ER	=	Education Rating
RDC	=	Rate Division Class
CA	=	Compensation Analysis
ARR(1)	=	Average Range Rate (1)
ARR(2)	=	Average Range Rate (2)
ARR(3)	=	Average Range Rate (3)
QR	=	Qualified Rate
CCW	=	Clergy Compensation Worksheet
MCCL	=	Maintain Current Compensation Level

Explanation of Applied Terms

Salary: Refers to the annual amount paid to full-time employees. Part-time salaries were deleted. Included in salary are any differentials, cost-of-living, and incentive earnings, only if regularly paid each pay period. Does not include overtime, bonuses, or profit sharing arrangements that are paid on a quarterly, semi-annual, or annual basis.

Salary Range: The established minimum and maximum annual salaries (structural ranges) reported for the position.

Nonexempt Salary: Refers to category of employees eligible for overtime payment under the Fair Labor Standards Act.

Exempt Salary: Those administrative and professional employees exempt from overtime payment under the Fair Labor Standards Act.

Explanation of Applied Terms
(continued)

General Increase: Any across the board increase granted to all or most employees in the group may sometimes be referred to as an Economic Adjustment.

COLA: (Cost of Living Allowance): An increase which is automatically granted to all employees in the group when the Consumer Price Index rises a given number of points. Such increase is usually granted in terms of cents per hour per month but for the purpose of this report is expressed as a percentage based on the average salary of the applicable group.

Merit Budget: The amount usually set by management as a percentage of payroll to be granted as salary merit increases during a year. Otherwise, the budget percentage is calculated as the sum of all merit increases granted (or scheduled to be granted in the year) divided by the total salaries of all eligible employees. This is irrespective of whether or not they received a merit increase.

Three Factors Used To Determine Compensation

1. Revenue Ratio
2. Quality Index - Based on Church Survey
3. Capacity to Pay - Based on Net Surplus

Revenue Ratio is the method used to compare the total revenue of the organization to a percentage that has been predetermined for the size ministry. Recommendations for annual compensation are based on ministry annual revenues. The range compensation should be tied to the Revenue Ratio. It needs to be noted this may not be a conclusive method for the benefit of the individuals receiving the compensation because it tends to be somewhat lower.

Quality Index would be determined either annually or bi-annually through a survey of the members of your church or organization. This will vary greatly depending on the size of a church or organization. (A sample of the membership could be surveyed rather than the entire membership.) This survey would result in what we refer to as a Quality Index which would determine where within the income range dictated by the Revenue Ratio you should be compensated in both salary and bonus. The higher your rating on the Quality Index (the church survey), the higher your compensation range would be.

Capacity to Pay will determine the extent which you could be paid at the maximum for which you qualify based on the Revenue Ratio and the Quality Index. For example, if your salary is $225,000 but you should be paid $250,000 based on the Revenue Ratio and the Quality Index, then you could be paid a bonus of $25,000 to produce the desired level of annual cash compensation.

After much survey and study, Michael Chitwood has determined that every organization or church needs to have a program that can be outlined so that a compensation designed plan can be put into place that would work in determining the appropriate compensation level for each individual. Remember, the Revenue Ratio range specified is the most commonly used because it requires less work. It also allows you to identify other factors if you're interested in performing the surveys and the analysis as described. Mr. Chitwood believes it's important that an individual or firm have an independent study of its compensation from the day-to-day administration that (1) determine the programs and guidelines which will govern compensation and (2) provide counsel and guidance in determining appropriate compensation levels for all personnel. It is extremely important that you have some verification of the compensation that's paid to key people in your ministry.

Factors in Determining the Level of Support

Budget planning and personnel committees are asked to consider the following factors in their annual review of support for the minister.

1. The Cost of Supporting the Minister's Family

What does it cost to maintain an adequate standard of living in this community? Family size, age of children and unique family needs must be taken into account.

2. Competence of the Minister

Many elements are involved in the competence of the minister; native ability, understanding of the ministry, education, experience, commitment, and Christian character.

3. Merit

How well does the minister do the job? Ministers who serve faithfully and effectively should receive merit increases which exceed cost of living adjustments.

4. Inflation

An annual increase at least large enough to offset the increase in consumer prices is necessary. Determine whether increases in recent years have kept pace, and if not, consider an adjustment and review together periodically, in order to maintain on a continuing basis the best possible arrangement for both.

The Bureau of Labor Consumer Price Index for recent years indicates the following percentage of increase:

1985	1986	1987	1988	1989	1990	1991	1992	1993	1994
3.8	1.1	4.4	4.4	4.6	6.1	3.1	2.9	2.7	2.5

1995	1996	1997	1998	1999	2000	2001	2002	2003	2004
3.3	1.7	1.6	2.7	3.4	1.6	2.4	1.6	3.4	3.5

5. Income of Other Professionals

Income of other professionals in the area of similar education and responsibility will provide another realistic guideline.

6. The Average Income of the Church Families

Socio-economic conditions of church communities vary greatly. Median per household "effective buying income" ranged from $9,105 to $24,010. The pastor's support should at least equal the average family in the church.

7. Ability of the Church to Support the Minister

The church cannot support the minister beyond its ability. The amount of income and giving potential of the members will determine what the church can actually do. The Benefit Commission recommends that each church begin using the suggested categories: Direct Income, Benefits, and Ministry Expense to determine Minister Salary Ranges.

8. Part-time Ministers

The recommended minimums should be adjusted in situations where the minister serves on a part-time basis.

Categories of Support

Churches should make a clear distinction between (1) ministry related expense, (2) fringe benefits, (3) direct personal income and (4) housing allowance.

1. Ministry Related Expense

Travel, conventions, continuing education, books, airfare, meals, lodging, gasoline, vestments, tapes, educational material and enterainment of guests are ministry related (business) expenses and should not be regarded as income for the minister.

It is important that the church budget reflect these distinct categories if the minister is to recieve maximum benefit from the support package by the church.

2. Fringe Benefits

Fringe benefits include group life insurance, disability insurance, medical insurance, retirement annuity, TSA, TDA, deferred compensation, 401(k), equity sharing, and split dollar. Provision for these benefits should be standard procedure for church committees considering the support of their ministers.

For the employees of the church, the General Convention recommends:

a. The church participate in a retirment program, depositing an amount equal to 10% of each employee's total compensation.

b. The church provide life, disability, and medical insurance protection for each full-time employee, furnishing at least one-half of the premium cost as an employee benefit.

c. The church consider other annuity, and mutual retirement funds.

3. Personal Income

Personal income for ministers includes base support, housing allowance and utilities allowance. The church will want to provide adequate personal income so that concern for financial needs does not detract from an effective ministry.

4. Housing Allowance

Recognizing that many churches do not own a parsonage, Congress expanded the tax-exempt housing concept to include property designated payments by a church to its minister with which he provides his own housing. This means that the amount expended by the minister for (a) rent and utilities, if renting a home, or (b) the principle interest, taxes, and utilities, if purchasing a home, is tax-free income so long as the amounts are properly designated by the church as housing allowance payments prior to the beginning of such allowance, and are actually for the authorized purposes. Even with no salary increase, a significant part of a minister's earnings can be converted to tax-free income through proper action by the church.
(Check each tax year for proper determination of housing allowance.)

Deferred Housing

Relatively new on the scene is an arrangement referred to as a deferred housing annuity. This is a fund created and maintained by the church for the purpose of accumulating a sum of money for the purchase of housing for the pastor at retirement. The minister has no control over this fund in the interim and thus he realizes no taxable income prior to maturity of the annuity.

It is important not only that both minister and church be aware of the possibilities in the area of housing for the minister, but also, that they plan.

Practical Application of Facts

The compensation information reported in this survey will help you make the data current anytime. Follow this technique:

Decide upon a percentage increase rate. This might be the overall projected increase of respondents, 6.0% or another figure you feel appropriate, say 10%.

Let's say you want to project salary levels for August 1. Since there are 10 months from October 1 to August 1, take 10/12ths of your projected annual increase. Example: 10/12 x .10 =.083.

Now, multiply the survey weighted averages by 1.083 to obtain the calendar-adjusted rate you want.

By using the procedure we'll describe now, you'll be able to develop a salary range around a desired midpoint (e.g. survey weighted average or percentage thereof):

Let the desired range spread be the symbol S
Let the desired salary range midpoint be the symbol MP

The salary range minimum may now be calculated using this formula:

$$\text{Minimum} = MP \left(1 - \frac{S}{2+S}\right)$$

And the salary range maximum may be calculated using this formula:

$$\text{Maximum} + (1 + S) \times \text{Minimum}$$

For example, if the desired range spread is 40% and the desired salary range midpoint is $10,000, the range minimum can be found this way:

Desired range spread = S = 40%

Salary range midpoint = MP = $10,000

$$\text{Minimum} = MP \left(1 - \frac{S}{2+S}\right)$$

$$= \$10,000 \, (1 - .4/2.4)$$

$$= \$10,000 \, (1 - 0.16)$$

$$= \$10,000 \, (.84)$$

$$\text{Minimum} = \$8,400$$

$$\text{Maximum} = (1 + S) \times \text{Minimum}$$

$$= 1.4 \times \$8,400$$

$$\text{Maximum} = \$11,760$$

Verify: 11,760/8,400 = 1.40, which means you have a salary range from $8,400 to $11,760 with a midpoint of $10,000 and a range of 40%.

Total Increase:

The sum of any combination of General, COLA, or Merit Increases.

Weighted Average Salary:

The average annual salary reported by the organization for a given position is multiplied by the number of employees in the job. The results are totaled for all organizations reporting the position and then divided by the total number of incumbents.

Average Range Minimum and Maximum:

The range salaries are added together and the total is divided by the number of entries.

Examples

Average	Weighted Average				
	Employees		Salary		
$18,300	3	x	18,300	=	$54,900
21,100	2	x	21,100	=	42,200
23,500	1	x	23,500	=	23,500
29,200	2	x	19,200	=	38,400
22,000	3	x	22,000	=	66,000
25,000	8	x	25,000	=	200,000
$139,100	19				$425,000

$139,100/6 = $23,183 $425,000/19 = $22,368

Average = $23,183   **Weighted Average = $22,368**

18

Annual Revenue and Geographic Displays

Data is displayed for organizations with annual revenue of under $500,000 and $1 million, for those with annual revenue of more than $1 million but less than $5 million, and for those with annual revenue of over $5 million. Within these categories, data are presented for six regions and for all regions combined. Finally, data for all organizations are combined for overall position average. Note: West Coast data does not include California which is reported as a separate region.

Regional data are only displayed where two or more organizations reported data, this is to protect confidentiality. However, data for all ministers was used for all the regions and combined totals.

The accompanying map of the United States illustrates the make-up by states of each region.

Regional Compensation Map

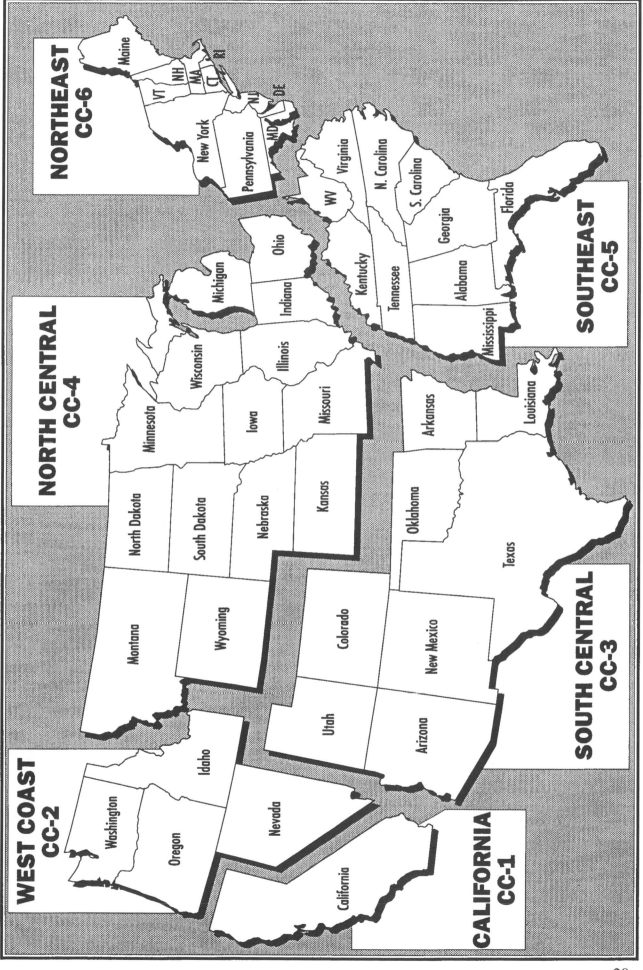

NORTHEAST CC-6

NORTH CENTRAL CC-4

WEST COAST CC-2

CALIFORNIA CC-1

SOUTH CENTRAL CC-3

SOUTHEAST CC-5

20

COMPENSATION GROUP OF AMERICA
COMPENSATION PACKAGE

REV.		DATE:	

		TOTALS
SALARY, BONUSES & OTHER DIRECT/EARNED COMPENSATION:		
	Salary for Services as Senior Pastor & Senior Executive Officer	
	Salary for Other Services: Chief Pilot	
	Salary for Other Services:	
	Christmas Bonus	
	Year-End & Birthday Bonus	
	Pay Advances	
	Other:	
	Other:	
	Honoraria for Outside Speaking When Taken Through Church/Ministry Payroll	
	Ministers Housing Allowance	
TOTAL SALARY & OTHER DIRECT/EARNED COMPENSATION:		

DEFERRED COMPENSATION/RETIREMENT		
	403(b) Church Retirement Plan	
	401(k) Church Retirement Plan	
	Deferred Compensation (Rabbi Trust)	
	Other:	
	Other:	
TOTAL DEFERRED COMPENSATION:		

TAXABLE FRINGE BENEFITS:

	Personal Use of Auto	
	Auto Allowances Paid in Cash	
	Federal Income Tax Paid by Church	
	Travel Allowance - Personal	
	Clothing Allowance	
	Purchase & Cleaning of Clergy Suits & Vestments	
	Group Term Life Insurance (Over $50,000 Face Value)	
	Other Insurance Premiums Paid by the Church	
	House Cleaning Allowance	
	Vacations Paid by Church	
	School Tuition Paid by Church for Pastor's Children	
	Other: Personal Use of Church Aircraft	
	Other:	
	Other:	
	Other:	
	Other:	
	Other:	
	Value of Low-Interest Loans	
	Canceled/Forgiven Debt	
	Personal Expenses Paid by Church by Check or Credit Card	
	Property Purchased From the Church at a Bargain Price	
	Church Property Transferred in Kind	
	Pastor's Discretionary Fund	
	Severance Pay	
	Spouse's Travel Expenses	
TOTAL TAXABLE FRINGE BENEFITS		
TOTAL COMPENSATION FOR PURPOSES		

OF DETERMINING "REASONABLENESS"

OTHER INCOME NOT CONSIDERED IN DETERMINING "REASONABLENESS"	
ROYALTIES:	
Royalties for Services as Author & Lecturer	
Publishing Royalties	
HONORARIA RECEIVED FOR OUTSIDE SPEAKING WHEN NOT PAID THROUGH CHURCH/MINISTRY PAYROLL:	

NON-TAXABLE FRINGE BENEFITS:

Business Use of Church Auto	
Other On-the-Job Transportation (Aircraft)	
Travel on Church Business	
Reimbursement for Auto Expenses or @ $.31/Mile	
Church-Paid Health Insurance Premiums	
Church-Financed Accident & Health Plan	
Self-Funded Medical Reimbursement Plan	
Reimbursements for Out of Pocket Health Expenses	
Group Term Life Insurance (Up to $50,000 Face Amount)	
Disability Insurance	
Educational Assistance $5,250/Year	
Educational Expense Reimbursement	
Moving Expense Reimbursement or Moving Expenses Paid by the Church	
Child & Dependent Care Expenses to Enable Minister & Spouse to Attend Church Functions	
Child Care Expenses to Enable Minister & Spouse to Attend Church Functions	
Child Care Expenses Provided by On-Premise Church Daycare	

	"Cafeteria" Plan	
	Working Condition Fringe Benefits	
	De Minimus Fringe Benefits	
	Church Cafeteria/Meals at Less Than Fair Market	
	Meals on Premises	
	Staff Achievement Awards	
	Church-Provided Legal Services	
	No-Additional-Cost Services	
	Qualified Employee Discounts	
	Other: Clergy Vestments Purchase & Cleaning	
	Other:	
	Other:	
	Other:	
TOTAL NON-TAXABLE FRINGE BENEFITS:		

Housing Allowance Expenditure Certification

To: Board of Directors/Trustees

From: _____

Date: _____

        This is to certify that the undersigned, _____,
a duly ordained, commissioned, or licensed minister of the church performing services for the church in the
exercise of my ministry, presented to you a Request for Housing Allowance ("RHA"), for the year
20____. The previously submitted RHA requested housing allowance in the total amount of $_____.
Upon your approval of the RHA, I was paid my housing allowance in full, on a monthly basis, pursuant to
the terms and conditions of the RHA.

        This is to certify that the undersigned is aware of the requirements of Internal Revenue Code Reg.
1.107-1 (c) wherein a parsonage rental allowance must be included in a minister's gross income in the
taxable year in which the allowance is received to the extent that the allowance is not used by the minister
during the taxable year to rent or otherwise provide for a home.

        This is to further certify that the undersigned is aware that Section 107 of the Internal Revenue
Code of 1986, as amended, provides that in the case of a minister of the gospel, gross income does not
include... the rental allowance paid to him as part of his compensation, to the extent used by him to rent or
provide a home, and that such tax exclusion for a rental allowance is available only to the extent the allowance is so used. IRS Section 107; Reg. 1.107-1(a).

        The undersigned hereby represents and certifies, subject to the penalties of perjury, that I have
received my housing allowance in accordance with the applicable provisions of the Internal Revenue Code,
and Regulations thereunder, and have applied my allowance to or for qualified parsonage housing expenditures. I further certify that I am aware of my obligations to the church, and to the Internal Revenue Service,
to make full disclosure and to report properly for income tax purposes the extent to which any portion of
my housing allowance receipts was not applied to parsonage related housing expenditures during the year
in which I received such payment.

_____
(Signature)

Address of Parsonage/Minister's Home:

_____

_____

Minister's Social Security No. _____

Benefits of Housing Worksheet

1. Minister can still get a tax deduction for mortgage interest and real estate taxes.

2. Equity increases with tax free money if you spend all you receive.

3. Minister establishes a line of credit by having property in his name.

4. No one can ever take your home away.

EXAMPLE

Fact #1 ....Salary of Minister 45,000.00

Fact # 2 ....Housing Allowance........................32,400.00

Fact # 3 ....Property Taxes................................2,000.00

Fact # 4 ....Mortgage Interest...........................9,000.00

Fact # 5 ....Value of Residence 150,000.00

CASH FLOW ANALYSIS

Cash Input	32,400.00
Tax Saving (Tax Rate **36** %)................................	3,960.00
Equity Increase (**3** %).....................................	4,500.00

TOTAL Cash Advantage (1 Year)..	40,860.00
Average Life of Earning Year	40
TOTAL Cash Advantage (40 Years)	1,634,400.00

Compensation Objectives

Review and assess the appropriateness of compensation levels and practices as applied to three to five pastors of churches served by a strategic compensation group.

Prepare a formal report on this assessment outlining the findings and conclusions from our study.

Begin building a database of church pastor compensation levels/practices that could be used in similar reviews/assessments in future projects of a similar nature.

Compensation Approach

1. Design a survey questionnaire which will be used in collecting basic information pertinent to the engagement. This questionnaire would be relatively detailed in nature and address the following topics:

   - Compensation levels and practices for the past three years.
   - Revenues and expenses of the church for the past three years.
   - Membership loss/gain of the church over the past three years.
   - Contributions and bequests to the church over the past three years.
   - Scope and responsibilities of the pastor position.
   - Documentation of compensation programs/practices employed by the church.
   - Financial statements of the church for the past three years.
   - Other related topics.

2. Review completed questionnaires and begin to tabulate and analyze initial findings.

3. Review and discuss questionnaire findings as well as back-up documentation useful or relevant to the study.

4. Perform more in-depth analysis of compensation levels and practices, to include inter-church/pastor comparisons and assessment of the relationship of compensation increases/decreases to relevant factors (e.g., membership gains/losses, increases/decreases in contributions and bequests, etc.)

5. Prepare preliminary report on the findings, conclusions and recommendations from our study.

6. Prepare and submit a report in final form.

Church Membership Survey

Please indicate the extent to which you personally agree or disagree with each of the following statements. Circle only one for each statement.

	Strongly Agree	Agree	Neutral	Disagree	Strongly Disagree

Liturgy/Worship Services

		Strongly Agree	Agree	Neutral	Disagree	Strongly Disagree
1.	Our worship services are stimulating and thought provoking.	5	4	3	2	1
2.	I gain new insight into my relationship with God from our services.	5	4	3	2	1
3.	A major factor in my affiliation with the church is the quality of its liturgy/ worship services.	5	4	3	2	1
4.	I like the sermons I hear at our services.	5	4	3	2	1
5.	The sermon represents the high point of each service.	5	4	3	2	1
6.	Most sermons are inspirational and move me toward a closer relationship with the Lord.	5	4	3	2	1
7.	Much thought and preparation go into our worship services.	5	4	3	2	1
8.	The music at our worship service represents an important part of the service and a reason for my attendance.	5	4	3	2	1
9.	The music performed by the choir is excellent.	5	4	3	2	1
10.	The music in our services helps me enter into an attitude of praise and worship.	5	4	3	2	1
11.	Our worship services have become somewhat stagnant and need to be re-examined and improved.	5	4	3	2	1

Member/Volunteer Development

		Strongly Agree	Agree	Neutral	Disagree	Strongly Disagree
12.	I am more actively involved in this church than any I have attended previously.	5	4	3	2	1
13.	Our pastor does an excellent job of recruiting and utilizing members and volunteers.	5	4	3	2	1
14.	The membership of the church continues to grow through the efforts of the pastor and staff.	5	4	3	2	1
15.	Volunteers are active and involved in church activities.	5	4	3	2	1
16.	New members or volunteers can be obtained as needed for special events and projects.	5	4	3	2	1

17. If the members of the church were more actively involved in its programs and activities, we could be more effective as an organization and our membership would grow at a faster rate.　　5　4　3　2　1

18. Although we have much to offer as a church, little is known about our worship services and programs outside of the membership.　　5　4　3　2　1

Vision/Mission of the Church

19. I have a clear understanding of the vision/mission of the church as expressed by the pastor.　　5　4　3　2　1

20. I agree with the vision/mission and work to support it.　　5　4　3　2　1

21. The vision/mission of the church is in line with the New Testament and the teachings of Christ.　　5　4　3　2　1

22. The vision/mission of the church is what distinguishes it from others and makes it special.　　5　4　3　2　1

Special Programs/Services

23. The counseling skills and services of the pastor are viewed as excellent by members of the church.　　5　4　3　2　1

24. I have been personally helped by counseling from the pastor or members of the staff.　　5　4　3　2　1

25. In time of personal crisis (e.g., marital difficulties, loss of family member, illness, etc.), I would feel free to turn to the pastor and could rely on him for help.　　5　4　3　2　1

26. Our church has worked hard to provide special programs/services in order to better serve our members or the broader community (e.g., bus ministry, food bank, etc.).　　5　4　3　2　1

27. The church has done an excellent job of establishing a ministry and programs for our children (ages birth - 11).　　5　4　3　2　1

28. The church has done an excellent job of establishing a ministry and programs for our youth (ages 12 - 18).　　5　4　3　2　1

29. The church has taken special steps to establish religious education programs/services to increase our understanding of the Word of God.　　5　4　3　2　1

30. The sacerdotal functions performed by the pastor represent an impor-　　5　4　3　2　1

	Strongly Agree	Agree	Neutral	Disagree	Strongly Disagree

tant reason to remain involved with the church (e.g., baptism, marriage, communion, etc.).

31. The evangelical work performed by the pastor (and members of his staff) has been a major factor in the growth and reputation of the church. — 5 4 3 2 1

32. I believe our church would grow at a faster rate if we offered more/better programs and services. — 5 4 3 2 1

Financial/Administrative Resources

33. I am pleased with the church's use of the monetary contributions I provide. — 5 4 3 2 1

34. The pastor appears to manage the overhead costs of the church in a prudent manner. — 5 4 3 2 1

35. I have confidence in the pastor's ability to be responsive to the needs of the church and to the Word of the Lord in the administration of the church's assets. — 5 4 3 2 1

36. As the church grows in membership, I believe that more money should be spent on facilities and special services. — 5 4 3 2 1

37. I would contribute more to the church if I thought the money would be used wisely. — 5 4 3 2 1

Demographic Information

The following information will be used to statistically compare groups within the church. Your responses will be compiled with many others and summarized for analysis purposes. No individual responses will be made available to the pastor or the members of the staff. The information you provide in answering these questions, as well as those throughout this questionnaire, is completely confidential.

1. AGE (at last birthday)

_____a. Under 25   _____d. 45 to 54
_____b. 25 to 34   _____e. 55 to 64
_____c. 35 to 44   _____f. 65 and over

2. SEX   _____a. Male   _____b. Female

3. MARITAL STATUS

_____a. Married   _____d. Divorced

_____b. Single   _____e. Widowed

_____c. Separated

4. NUMBER OF CHILDREN

_____a. None   _____e. Four

_____b. One   _____f. Five

_____c. Two   _____g. Six or more

_____d. Three

5. OCCUPATIONAL STATUS

_____a. Professional

_____b. Manager - Corporation

_____c. Business Owner/Operator

_____d. White Collar/Office Employee

_____e. Blue Collar/Plant Employee

_____f. Government Employee

6. EDUCATIONAL LEVEL (Highest Level Achieved)

_____a. Grammar School   _____e. Two-Year College Degree

_____b. Some High School   _____f. Four-Year College Degree

_____c. High School Graduate _____g. Some Graduate School

_____d. Some College   _____h. Graduate Degree

7. ANNUAL FAMILY INCOME (Adult Wage Earners)

_____a. Under $10,000   _____e. $25,000 - $34,999

_____b. $10,000 - $14,999   _____f. $35,000 - $49,999

_____c. $15,000 - $19,999   _____g. $50,000 - $74,999

_____d. $20,000 - $24,999   _____h. $75,000 and above

8. OTHER INFORMATION

Please use the space below to provide additional comments, observations or suggestions which reflect your asssessment of the church and its importance to you.

_____

_____

_____

_____

_____

_____

_____

_____

Pastor Compensation Analysis

Preliminary Questionnaire

Please review this Preliminary Questionnaire and provide answers and/or supporting data to the questions or items listed below. Some of these questions/items are for you to begin thinking about now, but will be developed comprehensively during a due-diligence onsite review and interview to be conducted by a church compensation specialist.

This information and material will serve as the basis of analysis of the appropriate compensation of the pastor of the church, and as the basis upon which any adjustments to current compensation can be justified.

1. Nature, extent and scope of pastor's duties. History of pastor's position with church.

2. Size of church.
   (a) Average attendance
   (b) Enrolled membership
   (c) 1, 2, 3-year growth of membership/attendance

3. Size of church and operations.
   (a) Budget history
   (b) Balance sheet comparison
   (c) Extent of operations
   (d) Use of media
   (e) Types of services

4. Ratio of pastor's cash compensation to:
   (a) Gross revenues of church
   (b) Net income (before salary)
   (c) All other salaries paid

5. Structure of pastor's compensation:
   (a) Salary
   (b) Housing allowance/parsonage
   (c) Perquisites/benefits
   (d) Retirement
   (e) Auto, medical, etc.

6. Five year history of pastor's compensation.

7. Pastor's responsibility for church's inception and/or success.

8. Who is responsible for establishing compensation at church.

9. Evidence of under-compensation for pastor in prior years or beginning period of church.

10. Compensation paid to pastor by church in accordance with a plan which has been followed consistently by church over a period of years.

11. Prevailing economic conditions in community from which church derives its revenue base.

12. Value to church of inducement to pay pastor for loyalty and to remain with the church.

13. Consequence to pastor and church of current or future public disclosure of pastor's compensation level.

14. Examination of the financial condition of the church after payment of restructured pastor compensation.

15. Uniqueness and replaceability of pastor under current church structure.

16. Clergy support and delegation of responsibility opportunities for pastor under current church structure.

17. Extent to which pastor is responsible for or directly charged with the obligation of raising funds for the church or maintaining/increasing current levels of church revenues.

18. Relative success of church compared to churches of similar size with comparable histories.

19. Existence of a free-bargaining relationship between the pastor and the church's compensation setting authority.

20. If a typical church member were viewed as a corporate shareholder, would the current or proposed pastor's compensation level be fair, and would it permit the "shareholder" to earn a fair return on his equity?

21. Is the pastor's salary reasonably consistent with the established salary relationship for all paid church employees?

22. Does the church "out perform" other comparable churches during good and bad economic periods under the pastor's leadership?

23. Is there a scarcity of pastors with the particular qualifications and talents of the church's pastor?

24. To what extent is capital a significant revenue generating factor compared to the personal services of the pastor (or others) in the church's annual budget?

25. Is the church in debt or does it borrow funds frequently?

26. Is the pastor willing to consider use of employment agreement requiring repayment to church of any amounts of compensation determined by IRS to be unreasonable pursuant to nonappealable final judgment of tax court or U.S. District Court or in settlement with the IRS of any threat to church's tax-exempt status involving inurement arising from compensation payment to pastor?

Compensation Questionnaire

General Information:

Church Name:_____ Phone:_____

Street Address:_____

City_____ State _____ Zip_____

Name:_____ Title:_____

Tenure in Position: _____Years   _____Months

Church Size:

	Year	Year	Year
1. Enrolled Membership			
2. Attendance - Sunday Services[1]			
3. Attendance - Midweek Services[2]			
4. Baptisms Performed			
5. Gross Annual Revenues			
6. Assets Under Management			
7. Operating Budget			
8. Gross Salaries[3]			
9. Paid Staff Members			
10. Volunteers in Service			

Pastor Role:

Responsibilities	Hours Per Week	% of Time[4]
1. Development of funds (fund raising)		
2. Recruitment of members		
3. Recruitment, training & staff supervision		
4. Recruitment, training & volunteer supervision		
5. Counseling of members (e.g., marital & bereavement counseling, etc.)		
6. Conduct of membership training		
7. Development and communication of vision		
8. Preparation of sermons		
9. Conduct of evangelical work		
10. Conduct of television ministry		
11. Conduct of radio broadcast ministry		

[1] Average attendance at all services on Sunday
[2] Average attendance at all mid-week services
[3] Gross salaries paid to all personnel who work for the church
[4] Percentage of time in the normal cycle of the job (e.g., one year) devoted to this responsibility

Responsibilities	Hours Per Week	% of Time[4]
12. Performance or oversight of sacerdotal functions	_____	_____
13. Management/conduct of bus ministry	_____	_____
14. Management/conduct of food bank	_____	_____
15. Preparation of cassettes, videos, articles for books, articles for magazines, etc.	_____	_____
16. Other - please specify:_____	_____	_____
_____	_____	_____
_____	_____	_____
_____	_____	_____

Qualifications:

1. Education:

High School Graduate	❑	Master of Divinity degree	❑
1-2 yrs. College	❑	Ph.D. degree	❑
Bachelor's degree	❑	Doctor of Divinity degree	❑
Master's degree	❑	Other:_____	

2. Years in Ministry:

1-3 Years	❑	11-15 Years	❑
4-6 Years	❑	16 or more	❑
7-10 Years	❑		

Compensation History

	This Year[5]	Year 2	Year 3	Year 4
1. Annual Salary	_____	_____	_____	_____
2. Housing Allowance/Parsonage	_____	_____	_____	_____
3. Automobile Allowance	_____	_____	_____	_____
4. Bonus/Incentive Compensation[6]	_____	_____	_____	_____
5. Gross Income Reported to IRS (W-2 form)	N/A	_____	_____	_____

Compensation Administration:

1. Who, or which party, determines your compensation level?

❑ Board of Directors   ❑ Pastor

❑ Compensation Committee of Board   ❑ Other - Specify_____

❑ Other Committee of Board - Specify:_____

[4]Percentage of time in the normal cycle of the job (e.g., one year) devoted to this responsibility
[5]Estimated or actual annual salary
[6]Report any cash payments which represent special bonus or incentive compensation for special work, accomplishments or endeavors during the year. These payments should be recorded on the line associated with the year in which they were paid.

2. Is there a formal plan document that governs your compensation (e.g., formal agreement with the Board regarding compensation, etc.)?

   ❑ Yes   ❑ No

   Please explain:_____

   _____

   _____

3. Is there a "free-bargaining relationship" between you and the church's compensation setting authority?

   ❑ Yes   ❑ No

   Please explain:_____

   _____

   _____

4. Is there a formal, defined process for reviewing and adjusting your compensation periodically?

   ❑ Yes   ❑ No

   Please explain:_____

   _____

   _____

5. Do you use any outside advisor, consultant or other independent party to advise or make recommendations regarding compensation?

   ❑ Yes   ❑ No

   Please explain:_____

   _____

   _____

6. How frequently is your compensation reviewed and adjusted?
   - ❑ Annually
   - ❑ Every two years
   - ❑ As necessary/required
   - ❑ Other: (Please explain:)_____

   _____

Actual Increase By Category

Descriptions	General Increases		COLA		Merit Increase		Total Increase	
	No. Orgs.	%	No. Orgs.	%	No. Orgs.	%	No. Orgs.	%
Non-Exempt Salaried Employees	200	4.9	151	3.7	147	4.8	268	6.0
Exempt Salaried Employees	281	4.7	164	3.6	155	4.7	281	5.9
Officers/Executives	283	5.2	155	4.0	141	5.5	268	6.6
TOTAL AVERAGE		**4.9**		**3.7**		**5.0**		**6.2**

39

Projected Increases By Category

Descriptions	General Increases		COLA		Merit Increases		Total Increases	
	No. Orgs.	%	No. Orgs.	%	No. Orgs.	%	No. Orgs.	%
Non-Exempt Salaried Employees	204	5.0	120	3.7	135	4.9	254	5.9
Exempt Salaried Employees	216	5.1	128	3.6	140	4.8	263	5.6
Officers/ Executives	218	6.9	131	3.6	124	5.9	262	6.3
TOTAL AVERAGE		5.6		3.6		5.2		5.9

Salary Range Increases

Nonexempt: _____

Officer/Executive: _____

Exempt: _____

Overall: _____

40

Regional Clergy Compensation Data

Under $499,000 Annual Revenue

	Average Salary	Average Range Minimum	Average Range Maximum
California	57,866	12.9%	14.1%
West Coast*	43,740	11.2%	12.9%
South Central	33,900	14.0%	17.1%
North Central	31,579	11.2%	17.6%
Southeast	31,797	9.4%	17.7%
Northeast	35,400	9.1%	13.1%
Category Average	**39,047**	**11.3%**	**15.4%**

*Excluding California

41

Regional Clergy Compensation Data

$500,000 - $1 Million Annual Revenue

	Average Salary	Average Range Minimum	Average Range Maximum
California	103,680	11.6%	13.4%
West Coast*	87,300	11.4%	12.9%
South Central	107,529	9.9%	13.0%
North Central	109,788	11.6%	15.2%
Southeast	61,080	5.7%	11.9%
Northeast	70,800	7.1%	12.2%
Category Average	**90,029**	**9.5%**	**13.1%**

*Excluding California

42

Regional Clergy Compensation Data

$1 Million - $2.5 Million Annual Revenue

	Average Salary	Average Range Minimum	Average Range Maximum
California	150,060	5.7%	9.1%
West Coast*	119,880	4.8%	8.7%
South Central	124,550	5.1%	8.9%
North Central	137,940	6.0%	9.3%
Southeast	116,130	5.0%	11.4%
Northeast	123,870	5.2%	10.6%
Category Average	**128,730**	**5.3%**	**9.7%**

*Excluding California

43

Regional Clergy Compensation Data

$2.5 - $5 Million Annual Revenue

	Average Salary	Average Range Minimum	Average Range Maximum
California	243,900	5.6%	8.4%
West Coast*	175,164	4.9%	8.3%
South Central	219,690	5.2%	8.2%
North Central	203,160	5.9%	8.7%
Southeast	180,300	5.2%	9.5%
Northeast	188,820	5.3%	9.0%
Category Average	**201,839**	**5.3%**	**8.7%**

*Excluding California

44

Regional Clergy Compensation Data

Over $5 Million Annual Revenue

	Average Salary	Average Range Minimum	Average Range Maximum
California	348,000	5.6%	7.7%
West Coast*	232,200	4.9%	7.8%
South Central	322,800	5.2%	7.6%
North Central	274,800	5.9%	8.1%
Southeast	253,740	5.4%	7.6%
Northeast	261,600	5.3%	7.4%
Category Average	**282,190**	**5.4%**	**7.7%**

*Excluding California

45

Regional Administrator Compensation Data

$250,000 to $499,000 Annual Revenue

	Average Salary	Average Range Minimum	Average Range Maximum
California	24,425	4.7%	6.4%
West Coast*	18,118	4.1%	5.8%
South Central	11,860	5.2%	7.7%
North Central	11,700	4.1%	7.9%
Southeast	9,850	3.5%	8.0%
Northeast	9,950	3.4%	5.9%
Category Average	**14,317**	**4.2%**	**7.0%**

*Excluding California

46

Regional Administrator Compensation Data

$500,000 - $1 Million Annual Revenue

	Average Salary	Average Range Minimum	Average Range Maximum
California	39,200	4.3%	6.0%
West Coast*	37,250	4.2%	5.8%
South Central	35,950	3.7%	5.9%
North Central	36,900	4.3%	6.9%
Southeast	28,100	2.1%	5.4%
Northeast	30,960	2.6%	5.5%
Category Average	**34,726**	**5.2%**	**5.9%**

*Excluding California

47

Regional Administrator Compensation Data

$1 Million - $2.5 Million Annual Revenue

	Average Salary	Average Range Minimum	Average Range Maximum
California	43,700	2.1%	4.1%
West Coast*	39,900	1.7%	3.3%
South Central	37,450	1.8%	3.4%
North Central	40,950	2.2%	3.6%
Southeast	36,700	1.7%	3.4%
Northeast	39,100	1.9%	3.9%
Category Average	**39,633**	**1.9%**	**3.6%**

*Excluding California

48

Regional Administrator Compensation Data

$2.5 - $5 Million Annual Revenue

	Average Salary	Average Range Minimum	Average Range Maximum
California	52,125	2.1%	3.8%
West Coast*	43,000	1.8%	3.4%
South Central	43,880	1.9%	3.4%
North Central	48,850	2.2%	3.6%
Southeast	43,750	1.8%	3.4%
Northeast	46,900	1.9%	3.5%
Category Average	**46,417**	**2.0%**	**3.5%**

*Excluding California

49

Regional Administrator Compensation Data

Over $5 Million Annual Revenue

	Average Salary	Average Range Minimum	Average Range Maximum
California	62,575	2.1%	3.5%
West Coast*	51,000	1.8%	3.5%
South Central	52,500	1.9%	3.4%
North Central	59,110	2.2%	3.6%
Southeast	53,250	2.0%	3.4%
Northeast	56,900	1.9%	3.3%
Category Average	**55,889**	**2.0%**	**3.5%**

*Excluding California

50

Qualified Scale
California CC-1

Scale			Range Minimum	Range Maximum
1,000	to	50,000		
50,000	to	100,000		
100,000	to	250,000		
250,000	to	500,000		
500,000	to	700,000		
700,000	to	1,000,000		
1,000,000	to	2,000,000		
2,000,000	to	3,000,000		
3,000,000	to	5,000,000		
5,000,000	to	7,000,000		
7,000,000	to	8,000,000		
8,000,000	to	9,000,000		
9,000,000	to	10,000,000		

Qualified Scale
West Coast* CC-2

Scale			Range Minimum	Range Maximum
1,000	to	50,000		
50,000	to	100,000		
100,000	to	250,000		
250,000	to	500,000		
500,000	to	700,000		
700,000	to	1,000,000		
1,000,000	to	2,000,000		
2,000,000	to	3,000,000		
3,000,000	to	5,000,000		
5,000,000	to	7,000,000		
7,000,000	to	8,000,000		
8,000,000	to	9,000,000		
9,000,000	to	10,000,000		

*Excluding California

51

Qualified Scale
South Central CC-3

Scale			Range Minimum	Range Maximum
1,000	to	50,000		
50,000	to	100,000		
100,000	to	250,000		
250,000	to	500,000		
500,000	to	700,000		
700,000	to	1,000,000		
1,000,000	to	2,000,000		
2,000,000	to	3,000,000		
3,000,000	to	5,000,000		
5,000,000	to	7,000,000		
7,000,000	to	8,000,000		
8,000,000	to	9,000,000		
9,000,000	to	10,000,000		

Qualified Scale
North Central CC-4

Scale			Range Minimum	Range Maximum
1,000	to	50,000		
50,000	to	100,000		
100,000	to	250,000		
250,000	to	500,000		
500,000	to	700,000		
700,000	to	1,000,000		
1,000,000	to	2,000,000		
2,000,000	to	3,000,000		
3,000,000	to	5,000,000		
5,000,000	to	7,000,000		
7,000,000	to	8,000,000		
8,000,000	to	9,000,000		
9,000,000	to	10,000,000		

Qualified Scale
Southeast CC-5

Scale			Range Minimum	Range Maximum
1,000	to	50,000		
50,000	to	100,000		
100,000	to	250,000		
250,000	to	500,000		
500,000	to	700,000		
700,000	to	1,000,000		
1,000,000	to	2,000,000		
2,000,000	to	3,000,000		
3,000,000	to	5,000,000		
5,000,000	to	7,000,000		
7,000,000	to	8,000,000		
8,000,000	to	9,000,000		
9,000,000	to	10,000,000		

Qualified Scale
Northeast CC-6

Scale			Range Minimum	Range Maximum
1,000	to	50,000		
50,000	to	100,000		
100,000	to	250,000		
250,000	to	500,000		
500,000	to	700,000		
700,000	to	1,000,000		
1,000,000	to	2,000,000		
2,000,000	to	3,000,000		
3,000,000	to	5,000,000		
5,000,000	to	7,000,000		
7,000,000	to	8,000,000		
8,000,000	to	9,000,000		
9,000,000	to	10,000,000		

Categories of Support for the Minister

Category 1	Amount
_____ _____ _____	$
Category 2	
_____ _____ _____	$
Category 3	
_____ **ARM-** **ARM+** _____	$
Category 4	
_____ _____ _____	$
Total Package	$

Compensation Worksheet

Church: _____   Name: _____

Revenue From All Sources: _____   _____%
(Classified Funds)

Building Fund   (A)_____

Stewardship Fund   (B)_____

Missions (Foreign Only)   (C)_____

Total Classified Funds   _____   _____%

Qualified Adjusted Revenue _____   _____

Salaries and Wages   _____   _____%
(Classified Salary)

Staff (Excluding Pastor)   (A)_____   _____%

Administrators   (B)_____   _____%

General Personnel   (C)_____   _____%

Total Classified Salaries   _____   _____%

Qualified Adjusted Salaries _____   _____

Option (A)

QAS_____ ÷ by QAR_____	= _____ %
QAR_____ x QR_____	= CCW_____
CCW_____ ÷ QAR_____	= _____ %

Option (B)

QAS_____ ÷ by QAR_____	= _____ %
QAR_____ x QR_____	= CCW_____
CCW_____ ÷ QAR_____	= _____ %

Compensation Worksheet

Church: _____ Name: _____

Revenue From All Sources: _____ _____%
(Classified Funds)

Building Fund   (A)_____

Stewardship Fund   (B)_____

Missions (Foreign Only)   (C)_____

Total Classified Funds   _____ _____%

Qualified Adjusted Revenue _____ _____

Salaries and Wages   _____ _____%
(Classified Salary)

Staff (Excluding Pastor)   (A)_____ _____%

Administrators   (B)_____ _____%

General Personnel   (C)_____ _____%

Total Classified Salaries   _____ _____%

Qualified Adjusted Salaries _____ _____

Option (A)

QAS_____ ÷ by QAR_____ = _____%

QAR_____ x QR_____ = CCW_____

CCW_____ ÷ QAR_____ = _____%

Option (B)

QAS_____ ÷ by QAR_____ = _____%

QAR_____ x QR_____ = CCW_____

CCW_____ ÷ QAR_____ = _____%

Compensation Worksheet

Church: _____ Name: _____

Revenue From All Sources: _____ _____%
(Classified Funds)

Building Fund   (A)_____

Stewardship Fund   (B)_____

Missions (Foreign Only)   (C)_____

Total Classified Funds   _____ _____%

Qualified Adjusted Revenue _____ _____

Salaries and Wages   _____ _____%
(Classified Salary)

Staff (Excluding Pastor)   (A)_____ _____%

Administrators   (B)_____ _____%

General Personnel   (C)_____ _____%

Total Classified Salaries   _____ _____%

Qualified Adjusted Salaries _____ _____

Option (A)

QAS_____	÷ by QAR_____	= _____%
QAR_____	x QR_____	= CCW_____
CCW_____	÷ QAR_____	= _____%

Option (B)

QAS_____	÷ by QAR_____	= _____%
QAR_____	x QR_____	= CCW_____
CCW_____	÷ QAR_____	= _____%

Compensation Worksheet

Region_____

State Code_____

Regional Minimum Range_____% Regional Maximum Range_____%

Service Years_____ Annual Clergy Hours Performed_____

Salaries & Wages_____=_____ ÷ by

QAR_____=_____%

TOTAL Salaries & Wages   _____%

TOTAL Classified Salaries & Wages   _____%

TOTAL QAS   _____%

TOTAL Salaries & Wages (SW ÷ Y = %)   _____%

TOTAL Classified Salaries & Wages (CSW ÷ Y = %)   _____%

TOTAL QAS (QAS ÷ Y = %)   _____%

Classified Salary Percentage _____ ÷ by _____ = _____%

AR (-) M_____% + AR(+) M_____% = APR _____%

APR_____% ÷ by _____ = TAPR_____%

(A) Average Range Maximum Percentage   (1)_____%

(B) Average Range Percentage   (2)_____%

   Subtract B from A (enter difference)   _____%

   Note: If B is greater than A (**DO NOT COMPLETE**) the lower part

(C) Classified Salary Percentage   _____%

(D) Add Line B + Line C   _____%

(A)_____% + (B)_____% + (C)_____% = _____%

(1)_____% ÷ by _____ = (3)_____%
                (See Index Table Page 58)

Compensation Worksheet

Region_____

State Code_____

Regional Minimum Range_____% Regional Maximum Range_____%

Service Years_____ Annual Clergy Hours Performed_____

Salaries & Wages_____=_____ ÷ by

QAR_____=_____%

TOTAL Salaries & Wages	_____%
TOTAL Classified Salaries & Wages	_____%
TOTAL QAS	_____%
TOTAL Salaries & Wages (SW ÷ Y = %)	_____%
TOTAL Classified Salaries & Wages (CSW ÷ Y = %)	_____%
TOTAL QAS (QAS ÷ Y = %)	_____%

Classified Salary Percentage_____ ÷ by_____=_____%

AR (-) M_____% + AR(+) M_____% = APR_____%

APR_____% ÷ by_____ = TAPR_____%

(A) Average Range Maximum Percentage   (1)_____%

(B) Average Range Percentage   (2)_____%

   Subtract B from A (enter difference)   _____%

   Note: If B is greater than A (**DO NOT COMPLETE**) the lower part

(C) Classified Salary Percentage   _____%

(D) Add Line B + Line C   _____%

(A)_____% + (B)_____% + (C)_____% = _____%

(1)_____% ÷ by_____ = (3)_____%
                (See Index Table Page 58)

Compensation Worksheet

Region_____

State Code_____

Regional Minimum Range_____% Regional Maximum Range_____%

Service Years_____ Annual Clergy Hours Performed_____

Salaries & Wages_____ = _____ ÷ by

QAR_____ = _____ %

TOTAL Salaries & Wages   _____%

TOTAL Classified Salaries & Wages   _____%

TOTAL QAS   _____%

TOTAL Salaries & Wages (SW ÷ Y = %)   _____%

TOTAL Classified Salaries & Wages (CSW ÷ Y = %)   _____%

TOTAL QAS (QAS ÷ Y = %)   _____%

Classified Salary Percentage _____ ÷ by _____ = _____%

AR (-) M_____% + AR(+) M_____% = APR _____%

APR_____% ÷ by _____ = TAPR_____%

(A) Average Range Maximum Percentage   (1)_____%

(B) Average Range Percentage   (2)_____%

     Subtract B from A (enter difference)   _____%

     Note: If B is greater than A (**DO NOT COMPLETE**) the lower part

(C) Classified Salary Percentage   _____%

(D) Add Line B + Line C   _____%

(A)_____% + (B)_____% + (C)_____% = _____%

(1)_____% ÷ by _____ = (3)_____%
              (See Index Table Page 58)

Compensation Analysis Worksheet

ANALYSIS 1

QAR = (Y) _____ x AR(1)R _____ =

Compensation Analysis $_____

ANALYSIS 2

QAR = (Y) _____ x AR(2)R _____ =

Compensation Analysis $_____

ANALYSIS 3

QAR = (Y) _____ x AR(3)R _____ =

Compensation Analysis $_____

ANALYSIS(1)_____ + ANALYSIS(2)_____ + ANALYSIS(3)_____ =

TOTAL _____ ÷ 3 = AVERAGE COMPENSATION ANALYSIS _____

Compensation Analysis Worksheet

ANALYSIS 1

QAR = (Y) _____ x AR(1)R _____ =

Compensation Analysis $_____

ANALYSIS 2

QAR = (Y) _____ x AR(2)R _____ =

Compensation Analysis $_____

ANALYSIS 3

QAR = (Y) _____ x AR(3)R _____ =

Compensation Analysis $_____

ANALYSIS(1)_____ +ANALYSIS(2)_____ +ANALYSIS(3)_____ =

TOTAL _____ ÷ 3 = AVERAGE COMPENSATION ANALYSIS _____

Compensation Analysis Worksheet

ANALYSIS 1

QAR = (Y) _____ x AR(1)R _____ =

Compensation Analysis $_____

ANALYSIS 2

QAR = (Y) _____ x AR(2)R _____ =

Compensation Analysis $_____

ANALYSIS 3

QAR = (Y) _____ x AR(3)R _____ =

Compensation Analysis $_____

ANALYSIS(1)_____+ANALYSIS(2)_____+ANALYSIS(3)_____=

TOTAL _____ ÷ 3 = AVERAGE COMPENSATION ANALYSIS _____

63

AVERAGE RANGE MAXIMUM

AVERAGE RANGE PERCENT	7.4	7.6	7.7	7.8	8.7	8.9	9.1	9.3	10.6	11.4	11.9	12.2	12.9	13.0	13.1	13.4	14.1	15.2	17.1	17.6	17.7
4.8	6.1	6.2	6.25	6.30	6.75	6.85	6.95	7.05	7.7	8.1	8.35	8.5	8.85	8.9	8.95	9.1	9.45	10.0	10.9	11.2	11.2
4.9	6.15	6.25	6.3	6.35	6.8	6.9	7.0	7.05	7.75	8.15	8.4	8.55	8.9	8.95	9.0	9.15	9.5	10.0	11.0	11.2	11.3
5.0	6.2	6.3	6.35	6.4	6.8	6.9	7.0	7.1	7.75	8.15	8.45	8.6	8.95	9.0	9.05	9.2	9.55	10.1	11.0	11.2	11.3
5.1	6.25	6.35	6.40	6.45	6.85	6.95	7.05	7.15	7.8	8.2	8.45	8.6	9.0	9.05	9.1	9.25	9.6	10.2	11.1	11.3	11.4
5.2	6.3	6.4	6.45	6.5	6.90	7.0	7.1	7.2	7.85	8.25	8.5	8.65	9.0	9.05	9.1	9.25	9.65	10.2	11.1	11.4	11.4
5.3	6.35	6.45	6.5	6.55	6.95	7.05	7.15	7.25	7.9	8.3	8.55	8.7	9.05	9.1	9.15	9.3	9.65	10.2	11.2	11.4	11.5
5.4	6.4	6.5	6.55	6.6	7.0	7.1	7.2	7.3	7.95	8.35	8.6	8.75	9.1	9.15	9.2	9.35	9.7	10.3	11.2	11.5	11.5
5.6	6.5	6.6	6.65	6.7	7.05	7.15	7.25	7.35	8.0	8.4	8.65	8.8	9.15	9.2	9.25	9.4	9.75	10.3	11.3	11.5	11.6
5.7	6.55	6.65	6.7	6.75	7.15	7.25	7.35	7.45	8.10	8.5	8.75	8.9	9.25	9.3	9.35	9.5	9.85	10.4	11.4	11.6	11.7
5.9	6.65	6.75	6.8	6.85	7.2	7.3	7.4	7.5	8.15	8.55	8.8	8.95	9.3	9.35	9.4	9.55	9.9	10.5	11.4	11.7	11.7
6.0	6.7	6.8	6.85	6.9	7.3	7.4	7.5	7.6	8.25	8.65	8.9	9.05	9.4	9.45	9.5	9.65	10.0	10.6	11.5	11.8	11.8
7.1	7.25	7.35	7.4	7.45	7.35	7.45	7.55	7.65	8.3	8.7	8.95	9.1	9.45	9.5	9.55	9.7	10.1	10.6	11.6	11.8	11.9
9.1	8.25	8.35	8.4	8.45	7.9	8.0	8.1	8.2	8.85	9.25	9.5	9.65	10.0	10.1	10.1	10.3	10.6	11.2	12.1	12.4	12.4
9.4	8.4	8.5	8.55	8.6	8.9	9.0	9.1	9.2	9.85	10.3	10.5	10.7	11.0	11.1	11.1	11.3	11.6	12.2	13.1	13.4	13.4
9.9	8.65	8.75	8.8	8.85	9.05	9.15	9.25	9.35	10.0	10.4	10.7	10.8	11.2	11.2	11.3	11.4	11.8	12.3	13.3	13.5	13.6
11.2	9.3	9.4	9.45	9.5	9.4	9.5	9.6	9.6	10.3	10.7	10.9	11.1	11.4	11.5	11.5	11.7	12.0	12.6	13.5	13.8	13.8
11.4	9.4	9.5	9.55	9.6	9.95	10.1	10.2	10.3	10.9	11.3	11.6	11.7	12.1	12.1	12.2	12.3	12.7	13.2	14.2	14.4	14.5
11.6	9.5	9.6	9.65	9.7	10.1	10.2	10.3	10.4	11.0	11.4	11.7	11.8	12.2	12.2	12.3	12.5	12.8	13.3	14.2	14.5	14.6
12.9	9.5	9.6	9.65	9.7	10.2	10.3	10.4	10.5	11.1	11.5	11.8	11.9	12.3	12.3	12.4	12.5	12.9	13.4	14.4	14.6	14.7
14.0	10.2	10.3	10.3	10.4	10.8	10.9	11.0	11.1	11.8	12.2	12.4	12.6	12.9	12.9	13.0	13.2	13.5	14.1	15.0	15.3	15.3
14.0	10.7	10.8	10.9	10.9	11.4	11.5	11.6	11.7	12.3	12.7	12.9	13.1	13.5	13.5	13.6	13.7	14.1	14.6	15.6	15.8	15.9

Amount From Table ÷ _____ = _____ Index Coefficient

(1)

64

Salary Conversion Table

Annually	Monthly	Weekly	Hourly	Annually	Monthly	Weekly	Hourly
7000	583.33	134.62	3.365	12000	1000.00	230.77	5.769
7100	591.67	136.54	3.413	12100	1008.33	232.69	5.817
7200	600.00	138.46	3.462	12200	1016.67	234.62	5.865
7300	608.33	140.38	3.510	12300	1025.00	236.54	5.913
7400	616.67	142.31	3.558	12400	1033.33	238.46	5.962
7500	625.00	144.23	3.606	12500	1041.67	240.38	6.010
7600	633.33	146.15	3.654	12600	1050.00	242.31	6.058
7700	641.67	148.08	3.702	12700	1058.33	244.23	6.106
7800	650.00	150.00	3.750	12800	1066.67	246.15	6.154
7900	658.33	151.92	3.798	12900	1075.00	248.08	6.202
8000	666.67	153.85	3.846	13000	1083.33	250.00	6.250
8100	675.00	155.77	3.894	13100	1091.67	251.92	6.298
8200	683.33	157.69	3.942	13200	1100.00	253.85	6.346
8300	691.67	159.62	3.990	13300	1108.33	255.77	6.394
8400	700.00	161.54	4.038	13400	1116.67	257.69	6.442
8500	708.33	163.46	4.087	13500	1125.00	259.62	6.490
8600	716.67	165.38	4.135	13600	1133.33	261.54	6.538
8700	725.00	167.31	4.183	13700	1141.67	263.46	6.587
8800	733.33	169.23	4.231	13800	1150.00	265.38	6.635
8900	741.67	171.15	4.279	13900	1158.33	267.31	6.683
9000	750.00	173.08	4.327	14000	1166.67	269.23	6.731
9100	758.33	175.00	4.375	14100	1175.00	271.15	6.779
9200	766.67	176.92	4.423	14200	1183.33	273.08	6.827
9300	775.00	178.85	4.471	14300	1191.67	275.00	6.875
9400	783.33	180.77	4.519	14400	1200.00	276.92	6.923
9500	791.67	182.69	4.567	14500	1208.33	278.85	6.971
9600	800.00	184.62	4.615	14600	1216.67	280.77	7.019
9700	808.33	186.54	4.663	14700	1225.00	282.69	7.067
9800	816.67	188.46	4.712	14800	1233.33	284.62	7.115
9900	825.00	190.38	4.760	14900	1241.67	286.54	7.163
10000	833.33	192.31	4.808	15000	1250.00	288.46	7.212
10100	841.67	194.23	4.856	15100	1258.33	290.38	7.260
10200	850.00	196.15	4.904	15200	1266.67	292.31	7.308
10300	858.33	198.08	4.952	15300	1275.00	294.23	7.356
10400	866.67	200.00	5.000	15400	1283.33	296.15	7.404
10500	875.00	201.92	5.048	15500	1291.67	298.08	7.452
10600	883.33	203.85	5.096	15600	1300.00	300.00	7.500
10700	891.67	205.77	5.144	15700	1308.33	301.92	7.548
10800	900.00	207.69	5.192	15800	1316.67	303.85	7.596
10900	908.33	209.62	5.240	15900	1325.00	305.77	7.644
11000	916.67	211.54	5.288	16000	1333.33	307.69	7.692
11100	925.00	213.46	5.337	16100	1341.67	309.62	7.740
11200	933.33	215.38	5.385	16200	1350.00	311.54	7.788
11300	941.67	217.31	5.433	16300	1358.33	313.46	7.837
11400	950.00	219.23	5.481	16400	1366.67	315.38	7.885
11500	958.33	221.15	5.529	16500	1375.00	317.31	7.933
11600	966.67	223.08	5.577	16600	1383.33	319.23	7.981
11700	975.00	225.00	5.625	16700	1391.67	321.15	8.029
11800	983.33	226.92	5.673	16800	1400.00	323.08	8.077
11900	991.67	228.85	5.721	16900	1408.33	325.00	8.125

Salary Conversion Table

Annually	Monthly	Weekly	Hourly	Annually	Monthly	Weekly	Hourly
17000	1416.67	326.92	8.173	22000	1833.33	423.08	10.577
17100	1425.00	328.85	8.221	22100	1841.67	425.00	10.625
17200	1433.33	330.77	8.269	22200	1850.00	426.92	10.673
17300	1441.67	332.69	8.317	22300	1858.33	428.85	10.721
17400	1450.00	334.62	8.365	22400	1866.67	430.77	10.769
17500	1458.33	336.54	8.413	22500	1875.00	432.69	10.817
17600	1466.67	338.46	8.462	22600	1883.33	434.62	10.865
17700	1475.00	340.38	8.510	22700	1891.67	436.54	10.913
17800	1483.33	342.31	8.558	22800	1900.00	438.46	10.962
17900	1491.67	344.23	8.606	22900	1908.33	440.38	11.010
18000	1500.00	346.15	8.654	23000	1916.67	442.31	11.058
18100	1508.33	348.08	8.702	23100	1925.00	444.23	11.106
18200	1516.67	350.00	8.750	23200	1933.33	446.15	11.154
18300	1525.00	351.92	8.798	23300	1941.67	448.08	11.202
18400	1533.33	353.85	8.846	23400	1950.00	450.00	11.250
18500	1541.67	355.77	8.894	23500	1958.33	451.92	11.298
18600	1550.00	357.69	8.942	23600	1966.67	453.85	11.346
18700	1558.33	359.62	8.990	23700	1975.00	455.77	11.394
18800	1566.67	361.54	9.038	23800	1983.33	457.69	11.442
18900	1575.00	363.46	9.087	23900	1991.67	459.62	11.490
19000	1583.33	365.38	9.135	24000	2000.00	461.54	11.538
19100	1591.67	367.31	9.183	24100	2008.33	463.46	11.587
19200	1600.00	369.23	9.231	24200	2016.67	465.38	11.635
19300	1608.33	371.15	9.279	24300	2025.00	467.31	11.683
19400	1616.67	373.08	9.327	24400	2033.33	469.23	11.731
19500	1625.00	375.00	9.375	24500	2041.67	471.15	11.779
19600	1633.33	376.92	9.423	24600	2050.00	473.08	11.827
19700	1641.67	378.85	9.471	24700	2058.33	475.00	11.875
19800	1650.00	380.77	9.519	24800	2066.67	476.92	11.923
19900	1658.33	382.69	9.567	24900	2075.00	478.85	11.971
20000	1666.67	384.62	9.615	25000	2083.33	480.77	12.019
20100	1675.00	386.54	9.663	25100	2091.67	482.69	12.067
20200	1683.33	388.46	9.712	25200	2100.00	484.62	12.115
20300	1691.67	390.38	9.760	25300	2108.33	486.54	12.163
20400	1700.00	392.31	9.808	25400	2116.67	488.46	12.212
20500	1708.33	394.23	9.856	25500	2125.00	490.38	12.260
20600	1716.67	396.15	9.904	25600	2133.33	492.31	12.308
20700	1725.00	398.08	9.952	25700	2141.67	494.23	12.356
20800	1733.33	400.00	10.000	25800	2150.00	496.15	12.404
20900	1741.67	401.92	10.048	25900	2158.33	498.08	12.452
21000	1750.00	403.85	10.096	26000	2166.67	500.00	12.500
21100	1758.33	405.77	10.144	26100	2175.00	501.92	12.548
21200	1766.67	407.69	10.192	26200	2183.33	503.85	12.596
21300	1775.00	409.62	10.240	26300	2191.67	505.77	12.644
21400	1783.33	411.54	10.288	26400	2200.00	507.69	12.692
21500	1791.67	413.46	10.337	26500	2208.33	509.62	12.740
21600	1800.00	415.38	10.385	26600	2216.67	511.54	12.788
21700	1808.33	417.31	10.433	26700	2225.00	513.46	12.837
21800	1816.67	419.23	10.481	26800	2233.33	515.38	12.885
21900	1825.00	421.15	10.529	26900	2241.67	517.31	12.933

Salary Conversion Table

Annually	Monthly	Weekly	Hourly	Annually	Monthly	Weekly	Hourly
27000	2250.00	519.23	12.981	32000	2666.67	615.38	15.385
27100	2258.33	521.15	13.029	32100	2675.00	617.31	15.433
27200	2266.67	523.08	13.077	32200	2683.33	619.23	15.481
27300	2275.00	525.00	13.125	32300	2691.67	621.15	15.529
27400	2283.33	526.92	13.173	32400	2700.00	623.08	15.577
27500	2291.67	528.85	13.221	32500	2708.33	625.00	15.625
27600	2300.00	530.77	13.269	32600	2716.67	626.92	15.673
27700	2308.33	532.69	13.317	32700	2725.00	628.85	15.721
27800	2316.67	532.62	13.365	32800	2733.33	630.77	15.769
27900	2325.00	536.54	13.413	32900	2741.67	632.69	15.817
28000	2333.33	538.46	13.462	33000	2750.00	634.62	15.865
28100	2341.67	540.38	13.510	33100	2758.33	636.54	15.913
28200	2350.00	542.31	13.558	33200	2766.67	638.46	15.962
28300	2358.33	544.23	13.606	33300	2775.00	640.38	16.010
28400	2366.67	546.15	13.654	33400	2783.33	642.31	16.058
28500	2375.00	548.08	13.702	33500	2791.67	644.23	16.106
28600	2383.33	550.00	13.750	33600	2800.00	646.15	16.154
28700	2391.67	551.92	13.798	33700	2808.33	648.08	16.202
28800	2400.00	553.82	13.846	33800	2816.67	650.00	16.250
28900	2408.33	555.77	13.894	33900	2325.00	651.92	16.298
29000	2416.67	557.69	13.942	34000	2833.33	653.85	16.346
29100	2425.00	559.62	13.990	34100	2841.67	655.77	16.394
29200	2433.33	561.54	14.038	34200	2850.00	657.69	16.442
29300	2441.67	563.46	14.087	34300	2858.33	659.62	16.490
29400	2450.00	565.38	14.135	34400	2866.67	661.54	16.538
29500	2458.33	567.31	14.183	34500	2875.00	663.46	16.587
29600	2466.67	569.23	14.231	34600	2883.33	665.38	16.635
29700	2475.00	571.15	14.279	34700	2891.67	667.31	16.683
29800	2483.33	573.08	14.327	34800	2900.00	669.23	16.731
29900	2491.67	575.00	14.375	34900	2908.33	671.15	16.779
30000	2500.00	576.92	14.423	35000	2916.67	673.08	16.827
30100	2508.33	578.85	14.471	35100	2925.00	675.00	16.875
30200	2516.67	580.77	14.519	35200	2933.33	676.92	16.923
30300	2525.00	582.69	14.567	35300	2941.67	678.85	16.971
30400	2533.33	584.62	14.615	35400	2950.00	680.77	17.019
30500	2541.67	586.54	14.663	35500	2958.33	682.69	17.067
30600	2550.00	588.46	14.712	35600	2966.67	684.62	17.115
30700	2558.33	590.38	14.760	35700	2975.00	686.54	17.163
30800	2566.67	592.31	14.808	35800	2983.33	688.46	17.212
30900	2575.00	594.23	14.856	35900	2991.67	690.38	17.260
31000	2583.33	596.15	14.904	36000	3000.00	692.31	17.308
31100	2591.67	598.08	14.952	36100	3008.33	694.23	17.356
31200	2600.00	600.00	15.000	36200	3016.67	696.15	17.434
31300	2608.33	601.92	15.048	36300	3025.00	698.08	17.452
31400	2616.67	603.85	15.096	36400	3033.33	700.00	17.500
31500	2625.00	605.77	15.144	36500	3041.67	701.92	17.548
31600	2633.33	607.69	15.192	36600	3050.00	703.85	17.596
31700	2641.67	609.62	15.240	36700	3058.33	705.77	17.644
31800	2650.00	611.54	15.288	36800	3066.67	707.69	17.692
31900	2658.33	613.46	15.337	36900	3075.00	709.62	17.740

Salary Conversion Table

Annually	Monthly	Weekly	Hourly	Annually	Monthly	Weekly	Hourly
37000	3083.33	711.54	17.788	42000	3500.00	807.69	20.192
37100	3091.67	713.46	17.837	42100	3508.33	809.62	20.240
37200	3100.00	715.38	17.885	42200	3516.67	811.54	20.288
37300	3108.33	717.31	17.933	42300	3525.00	813.46	20.337
37400	3116.67	719.23	17.981	42400	3533.33	815.38	20.385
37500	3125.00	721.15	18.029	42500	3541.67	817.31	20.433
37600	3133.33	723.08	18.077	42600	3550.00	819.23	20.481
37700	3141.67	725.00	18.125	42700	3558.33	821.15	20.529
37800	3150.00	726.92	18.173	42800	3566.67	823.08	20.577
37900	3158.33	728.85	18.221	42900	3575.00	825.00	20.625
38000	3166.67	730.77	18.269	43000	3583.33	826.92	20.673
38100	3175.00	732.69	18.317	43100	3591.67	828.85	20.721
38200	3183.33	734.62	18.365	43200	3600.00	830.77	20.769
38300	3191.67	736.54	18.413	43300	3608.33	832.69	20.817
38400	3200.00	738.46	18.462	43400	3616.67	834.62	20.865
38500	3208.33	740.38	18.510	43500	3625.00	836.54	20.913
38600	3216.67	742.31	18.558	43600	3633.33	838.46	20.962
38700	3225.00	744.23	18.606	43700	3641.67	840.38	21.010
38800	3233.33	746.15	18.654	43800	3650.00	842.31	21.058
38900	3241.67	748.08	18.702	43900	3658.33	844.23	21.106
39000	3250.00	750.00	18.750	44000	3666.67	846.15	21.154
39100	3258.33	751.92	18.798	44100	3675.00	848.08	21.202
39200	3266.67	753.85	18.846	44200	3683.33	850.00	21.250
39300	3275.00	755.77	18.894	44300	3691.67	881.92	21.298
39400	3283.33	757.69	18.942	44400	3700.00	853.85	21.346
39500	3291.67	759.62	18.990	44500	3708.33	855.77	21.394
39600	3300.00	761.54	19.038	44600	3716.67	857.69	21.442
39700	3308.33	763.46	19.087	44700	3725.00	859.62	21.490
39800	3316.67	765.38	19.135	44800	3733.33	861.54	21.538
39900	3325.00	767.31	19.183	44900	3741.67	863.46	21.587
40000	3333.33	769.23	19.231	45000	3750.00	865.38	21.635
40100	3341.67	771.15	19.279	45100	3758.33	867.31	21.683
40200	3350.00	773.08	19.327	45200	3766.67	869.23	21.731
40300	3358.33	775.00	19.375	45300	3775.00	871.15	21.779
40400	3366.67	776.92	19.423	45400	3783.33	873.08	21.827
40500	3375.00	778.85	19.471	45500	3791.67	875.00	21.875
40600	3383.33	780.77	19.519	45600	3800.00	876.92	21.923
40700	3391.67	782.69	19.567	45700	3808.33	878.85	21.971
40800	3400.00	784.62	19.615	45800	3816.67	880.77	22.019
40900	3408.33	786.54	19.663	45900	3825.00	882.69	22.067
41000	3416.67	788.46	19.712	46000	3833.33	884.62	22.115
41100	3425.00	790.38	19.760	46100	3841.67	886.54	22.163
41200	3433.33	792.31	19.808	46200	3850.00	888.46	22.212
41300	3441.67	794.23	19.856	46300	3858.33	890.38	22.260
41400	3450.00	796.15	19.904	46400	3866.67	892.31	22.308
41500	3458.33	798.08	19.952	46500	3875.00	894.23	22.356
41600	3466.67	800.00	20.000	46600	3883.33	896.15	22.404
41700	3475.00	801.92	20.048	46700	3891.67	898.08	22.452
41800	3483.33	803.85	20.096	46800	3900.00	900.00	22.500
41900	3491.67	805.77	20.144	46900	3908.33	901.92	22.548

Salary Conversion Table

Annually	Monthly	Weekly	Hourly		Annually	Monthly	Weekly	Hourly
47000	3916.67	903.85	22.596		52000	4333.33	1000.00	25.000
47100	3925.00	905.77	22.644		52100	4341.67	1001.92	25.048
47200	3933.33	907.69	22.692		52200	4350.00	1003.85	25.096
47300	3941.67	909.62	22.740		52300	4358.33	1005.77	25.144
47400	3950.00	911.54	22.788		52400	4366.67	1007.69	25.192
47500	3958.33	913.46	22.837		52500	4375.00	1009.62	25.240
47600	3966.67	915.38	22.885		52600	4383.33	1011.54	25.288
47700	3975.00	917.31	22.933		52700	4391.67	1013.46	25.337
47800	3983.33	919.23	22.981		52800	4400.00	1015.38	25.385
47900	3991.67	921.15	23.029		52900	4408.33	1017.31	25.433
48000	4000.00	923.08	23.077		53000	4416.67	1019.23	25.481
48100	4008.33	925.00	23.125		53100	4425.00	1021.15	25.529
48200	4016.67	926.92	23.173		53200	4433.33	1023.08	25.577
48300	4025.00	928.85	23.221		53300	4441.67	1025.00	25.625
48400	4033.33	930.77	23.269		53400	4450.00	1026.92	25.673
48500	4041.67	932.69	23.317		53500	4458.33	1028.85	25.721
48600	4050.00	934.62	23.365		53600	4466.67	1030.77	25.769
48700	4058.33	936.54	23.413		53700	4475.00	1032.69	25.817
48800	4066.67	938.46	23.462		53800	4483.33	1034.62	25.865
48900	4075.00	940.38	23.510		53900	4491.67	1036.54	25.913
49000	4083.33	942.31	23.558		54000	4500.00	1038.46	25.962
49100	4091.67	944.23	23.606		54100	4508.33	1040.38	26.010
49200	4100.00	946.15	23.654		54200	4516.67	1042.31	26.058
49300	4108.33	948.08	23.702		54300	4525.00	1044.23	26.106
49400	4116.67	950.00	23.750		54400	4533.33	1046.15	26.154
49500	4125.00	951.92	23.798		54500	4541.67	1048.08	26.202
49600	4133.33	953.85	23.846		54600	4550.00	1050.00	26.250
49700	4141.67	955.77	23.894		54700	4558.33	1051.92	26.298
49800	4150.00	957.69	23.942		54800	4566.67	1053.85	26.346
49900	4158.33	959.62	23.990		54900	4575.00	1055.77	26.394
50000	4166.67	961.54	24.038		55000	4583.33	1057.69	26.442
50100	4175.00	963.46	24.087		55100	4591.67	1059.62	26.490
50200	4183.33	965.38	24.135		55200	4600.00	1061.54	26.538
50300	4191.67	967.31	24.183		55300	4608.33	1063.46	26.587
50400	4200.00	969.23	24.231		55400	4616.67	1065.38	26.635
50500	4208.33	971.15	24.279		55500	4625.00	1067.31	26.683
50600	4216.67	973.08	24.327		55600	4633.33	1069.23	26.731
50700	4225.00	975.00	24.375		55700	4641.67	1071.15	26.779
50800	4233.33	976.92	24.423		55800	4650.00	1073.08	26.827
50900	4241.67	978.85	24.471		55900	4658.33	1075.00	26.875
51000	4250.00	980.77	24.519		56000	4666.67	1076.92	26.923
51100	4258.33	982.69	24.567		56100	4675.00	1078.85	26.971
51200	4266.67	984.62	24.615		56200	4683.33	1080.77	27.019
51300	4275.00	986.54	24.663		56300	4691.67	1082.69	27.067
51400	4283.33	988.46	24.712		56400	4700.00	1084.62	27.115
51500	4291.67	990.38	24.760		56500	4708.33	1086.54	27.163
51600	4300.00	992.31	24.808		56600	4716.67	1088.46	27.212
51700	4308.33	994.23	24.856		56700	4725.00	1090.38	27.260
51800	4316.67	996.15	24.904		56800	4733.33	1092.31	27.308
51900	4325.00	998.08	24.952		56900	4741.67	1094.23	27.356

Salary Conversion Table

Annually	Monthly	Weekly	Hourly	Annually	Monthly	Weekly	Hourly
57000	4750.00	1096.15	27.404	62000	5166.67	1192.31	29.808
57100	4758.33	1098.08	27.452	62100	5175.00	1194.23	29.856
57200	4766.67	1100.00	27.500	62200	5183.33	1196.15	29.904
57300	4775.00	1101.92	27.548	62300	5191.67	1198.08	29.952
57400	4783.33	1103.85	27.596	62400	5200.00	1200.00	30.000
57500	4791.67	1105.77	27.644	62500	5208.33	1201.92	30.048
57600	4800.00	1107.69	27.692	62600	5216.67	1203.85	30.096
57700	4808.33	1109.62	27.740	62700	5225.00	1205.77	30.144
57800	4816.67	1111.54	27.788	62800	5233.33	1207.69	30.192
57900	4825.00	1113.46	27.837	62900	5241.67	1209.62	30.240
58000	4833.33	1115.38	27.885	63000	5250.00	1211.54	30.288
58100	4841.67	1117.31	27.933	63100	5258.33	1213.46	30.337
58200	4850.00	1119.23	27.981	63200	5266.67	1215.38	30.385
58300	4858.33	1121.15	28.029	63300	5275.00	1217.31	30.433
58400	4866.67	1123.08	28.077	63400	5283.33	1219.23	30.481
58500	4875.00	1125.00	28.125	63500	5291.67	1221.15	30.529
58600	4883.33	1126.92	28.173	63600	5300.00	1223.08	30.577
58700	4891.67	1128.85	28.221	63700	5308.33	1225.00	30.625
58800	4900.00	1130.77	28.269	63800	5316.67	1226.92	30.673
58900	4908.33	1132.69	28.317	63900	5325.00	1228.85	30.721
59000	4916.67	1134.62	28.365	64000	5333.33	1230.77	30.769
59100	4925.00	1136.54	28.413	64100	5341.67	1232.69	30.817
59200	4933.33	1138.46	28.462	64200	5350.00	1234.62	30.865
59300	4941.67	1140.38	28.510	64300	5358.33	1236.54	30.913
59400	4950.00	1142.31	28.558	64400	5366.67	1238.46	30.962
59500	4958.33	1144.23	28.606	64500	5375.00	1240.38	31.010
59600	4966.67	1146.15	28.654	64600	5383.33	1242.31	31.058
59700	4975.00	1148.08	28.702	64700	5391.67	1244.23	31.106
59800	4983.33	1150.00	28.750	64800	5400.00	1246.15	31.154
59900	4991.67	1151.92	28.798	64900	5408.33	1248.08	31.202
60000	5000.00	1153.85	28.846	65000	5416.67	1250.00	31.250
60100	5008.33	1155.77	28.894	65100	5425.00	1251.92	31.298
60200	5016.67	1157.69	28.942	65200	5433.33	1253.85	31.346
60300	5025.00	1159.62	28.990	65300	5441.67	1255.77	31.394
60400	5033.33	1161.54	29.038	65400	5450.00	1257.69	31.442
60500	5041.67	1163.46	29.087	65500	5458.33	1259.62	31.490
60600	5050.00	1165.38	29.135	65600	5466.67	1261.54	31.538
60700	5058.33	1167.31	29.183	65700	5475.00	1263.46	31.587
60800	5066.67	1169.23	29.231	65800	5483.33	1265.38	31.635
60900	5075.00	1171.15	29.279	65900	5491.67	1267.31	31.683
61000	5083.33	1173.08	29.327	66000	5500.00	1269.23	31.731
61100	5091.67	1175.00	29.375	66100	5508.33	1271.15	31.779
61200	5100.00	1176.92	29.423	66200	5516.67	1273.08	31.827
61300	5108.33	1178.85	29.471	66300	5525.00	1275.00	31.875
61400	5116.67	1180.77	29.519	66400	5533.33	1276.92	31.923
61500	5125.00	1182.69	29.567	66500	5541.67	1278.85	31.971
61600	5133.33	1184.62	29.615	66600	5550.00	1280.77	32.019
61700	5141.67	1186.54	29.663	66700	5558.33	1282.69	32.067
61800	5150.00	1188.46	29.712	66800	5566.67	1284.62	32.115
61900	5158.33	1190.38	29.760	66900	5575.00	1286.54	32.163

Salary Conversion Table

Annually	Monthly	Weekly	Hourly	Annually	Monthly	Weekly	Hourly
67000	5583.33	1288.46	32.212	72000	6000.00	1384.62	34.615
67100	5591.67	1290.38	32.260	72100	6008.33	1386.54	34.663
67200	5600.00	1292.31	32.308	72200	6016.67	1388.46	34.712
67300	5608.33	1294.23	32.356	72300	6025.00	1390.38	34.760
67400	5616.67	1296.15	32.404	72400	6033.33	1392.31	34.808
67500	5625.00	1298.08	32.452	72500	6041.67	1394.23	34.856
67600	5633.33	1300.00	32.500	72600	6050.00	1396.15	34.904
67700	5641.67	1301.92	32.548	72700	6058.33	1398.08	34.952
67800	5650.00	1303.85	32.596	72800	6066.67	1400.00	35.000
67900	5658.33	1305.77	32.644	72900	6075.00	1401.92	35.048
68000	5666.67	1307.69	32.692	73000	6083.33	1403.85	35.096
68100	5675.00	1309.62	32.740	73100	6091.67	1405.77	35.144
68200	5683.33	1311.54	32.788	73200	6100.00	1407.69	35.192
68300	5691.67	1313.46	32.837	73300	6108.33	1409.62	35.240
68400	5700.00	1315.38	32.885	73400	6116.67	1411.54	35.288
68500	5708.33	1317.31	32.933	73500	6125.00	1413.46	35.337
68600	5716.67	1319.23	32.981	73600	6133.33	1415.38	35.385
68700	5725.00	1321.15	33.029	73700	6141.67	1417.31	35.433
68800	5733.33	1323.08	33.077	73800	6150.00	1419.23	35.481
68900	5741.67	1325.00	33.125	73900	6158.33	1421.15	35.529
69000	5750.00	1326.92	33.173	74000	6166.67	1423.08	35.577
69100	5758.33	1328.85	33.221	74100	6175.00	1425.00	35.625
69200	5766.67	1330.77	33.269	74200	6183.33	1426.92	35.673
69300	5775.00	1332.69	33.317	74300	6191.67	1428.85	35.721
69400	5783.33	1334.62	33.365	74400	6200.00	1430.77	35.769
69500	5791.67	1336.54	33.413	74500	6208.33	1432.69	35.817
69600	5800.00	1338.46	33.462	74600	6216.67	1434.62	35.865
69700	5808.33	1340.38	33.510	74700	6225.00	1436.54	35.913
69800	5816.67	1342.31	33.558	74800	6233.33	1438.46	35.962
69900	5825.00	1344.23	33.606	74900	6241.67	1440.38	36.010
70000	5833.33	1346.15	33.654	75000	6250.00	1442.31	36.058
70100	5841.67	1348.08	33.702	75100	6258.33	1444.23	36.106
70200	5850.00	1350.00	33.750	75200	6266.67	1446.15	36.154
70300	5858.33	1351.92	33.798	75300	6275.00	1448.08	36.202
70400	5866.67	1353.85	33.846	75400	6283.33	1450.00	36.250
70500	5875.00	1355.77	33.894	75500	6291.67	1451.92	36.298
70600	5883.33	1357.69	33.942	75600	6300.00	1453.85	36.346
70700	5891.67	1359.62	33.990	75700	6308.33	1455.77	36.394
70800	5900.00	1361.54	34.038	75800	6316.67	1547.69	36.442
70900	5908.33	1363.46	34.087	75900	6325.00	1459.62	36.490
71000	5916.67	1365.38	34.135	76000	6333.33	1461.54	36.538
71100	5925.00	1367.31	34.183	76100	6341.67	1463.46	36.587
71200	5933.33	1369.23	34.231	76200	6350.00	1465.38	36.635
71300	5941.67	1371.15	34.279	76300	6358.33	1467.31	36.683
71400	5950.00	1373.08	34.327	76400	6366.67	1469.23	36.731
71500	5958.33	1375.00	34.375	76500	6375.00	1471.15	36.779
71600	5966.67	1376.92	34.423	76600	6383.33	1473.08	36.827
71700	5975.00	1378.85	34.471	76700	6391.67	1475.00	36.875
71800	5983.33	1380.77	34.519	76800	6400.00	1476.92	36.923
71900	5991.67	1382.69	34.567	76900	6408.33	1478.85	36.971

Salary Conversion Table

Annually	Monthly	Weekly	Hourly	Annually	Monthly	Weekly	Hourly
77000	6416.67	1480.77	37.019	82000	6833.33	1576.92	39.423
77100	6425.00	1482.69	37.067	82100	6841.67	1578.85	39.471
77200	6433.33	1484.62	37.115	82200	6850.00	1580.77	39.519
77300	6441.67	1486.54	37.163	82300	6858.33	1582.69	39.567
77400	6450.00	1488.46	37.212	82400	6866.67	1584.62	39.615
77500	6458.33	1490.38	37.260	82500	6875.00	1586.54	39.663
77600	6466.67	1492.31	37.308	82600	6883.33	1588.46	39.712
77700	6475.00	1494.23	37.356	82700	6891.67	1590.38	39.760
77800	6483.33	1496.15	37.404	82800	6900.00	1592.31	39.808
77900	6491.67	1498.08	37.452	82900	6908.33	1594.23	39.856
78000	6500.00	1500.00	37.500	83000	6916.67	1596.15	39.904
78100	6508.33	1501.92	37.548	83100	6925.00	1598.08	39.952
78200	6516.67	1503.85	37.596	83200	6933.33	1600.00	40.000
78300	6525.00	1505.77	37.644	83300	6941.67	1601.92	40.048
78400	6533.33	1507.69	37.692	83400	6950.00	1603.85	40.096
78500	6541.67	1509.62	37.740	83500	6958.33	1605.77	40.144
78600	6550.00	1511.54	37.788	83600	6966.67	1607.69	40.192
78700	6558.33	1513.46	37.837	83700	6975.00	1609.62	40.240
78800	6566.67	1515.38	37.885	83800	6983.33	1611.54	40.288
78900	6575.00	1517.31	37.933	83900	6991.67	1613.46	40.337
79000	6583.33	1519.23	37.981	84000	7000.00	1615.38	40.385
79100	6591.67	1521.15	38.029	84100	7008.33	1617.31	40.433
79200	6600.00	1523.08	38.077	84200	7016.67	1619.23	40.481
79300	6608.33	1525.00	38.125	84300	7025.00	1621.15	40.529
79400	6616.67	1526.92	38.173	84400	7033.33	1623.08	40.577
79500	6625.00	1528.85	38.221	84500	7041.67	1625.00	40.625
79600	6633.33	1530.77	38.269	84600	7050.00	1626.92	40.673
79700	6641.67	1532.69	38.317	84700	7058.33	1628.85	40.721
79800	6650.00	1534.62	38.365	84800	7066.67	1630.77	40.769
79900	6658.33	1536.54	38.413	84900	7075.00	1632.69	40.817
80000	6666.67	1538.46	38.462	85000	7083.33	1634.62	40.865
80100	6675.00	1540.38	38.510	85100	7091.67	1636.54	40.913
80200	6683.33	1542.31	38.558	85200	7100.00	1638.46	40.962
80300	6691.67	1544.23	38.606	85300	7108.33	1640.38	41.010
80400	6700.00	1546.15	38.654	85400	7116.67	1642.31	41.058
80500	6708.33	1548.08	38.702	85500	7125.00	1644.23	41.106
80600	6716.67	1550.00	38.750	85600	7133.33	1646.15	41.154
80700	6725.00	1551.92	38.798	85700	7141.67	1648.08	41.202
80800	6733.33	1553.85	38.846	85800	7150.00	1650.00	41.250
80900	6741.67	1555.77	38.894	85900	7158.33	1651.92	41.298
81000	6750.00	1557.69	38.942	86000	7166.67	1653.85	41.346
81100	6758.33	1559.62	38.990	86100	7175.00	1655.77	41.394
81200	6766.67	1561.54	39.038	86200	7183.33	1657.69	41.442
81300	6775.00	1563.46	39.087	86300	7191.67	1659.62	41.490
81400	6783.33	1565.38	39.135	86400	7200.00	1661.54	41.538
81500	6791.67	1567.31	39.183	86500	7208.33	1663.46	41.587
81600	6800.00	1569.23	39.231	86600	7216.67	1665.38	41.635
81700	6808.33	1571.15	39.279	86700	7225.00	1667.31	41.683
81800	6816.67	1573.08	39.327	86800	7233.33	1669.23	41.731
81900	6825.00	1575.00	39.375	86900	7241.67	1671.15	41.779

Salary Conversion Table

Annually	Monthly	Weekly	Hourly	Annually	Monthly	Weekly	Hourly
87000	7250.00	1673.08	41.827	92000	7666.67	1769.23	44.231
87100	7258.33	1675.00	41.875	92100	7675.00	1771.15	44.279
87200	7266.67	1676.92	41.923	92200	7683.33	1773.08	44.327
87300	7275.00	1678.85	41.971	92300	7691.67	1775.00	44.375
87400	7283.33	1680.77	41.019	92400	7700.00	1776.92	44.423
87500	7291.67	1682.69	42.067	92500	7708.33	1778.85	44.471
87600	7300.00	1684.62	42.115	92600	7716.67	1780.77	44.519
87700	7308.33	1686.54	42.163	92700	7725.00	1782.69	44.567
87800	7316.67	1688.46	42.212	92800	7733.33	1784.62	44.615
87900	7325.00	1690.38	42.260	92900	7741.67	1786.54	44.663
88000	7333.33	1692.31	42.308	93000	7750.00	1788.46	44.712
88100	7341.67	1694.23	42.356	93100	7758.33	1790.38	44.760
88200	7350.00	1696.15	42.404	93200	7766.67	1792.31	44.808
88300	7358.33	1698.08	42.452	93300	7775.00	1794.23	44.856
88400	7366.67	1700.00	42.500	93400	7783.33	1796.15	44.904
88500	7375.00	1701.92	42.548	93500	7791.67	1798.08	44.952
88600	7383.33	1703.85	42.596	93600	7800.00	1800.00	45.000
88700	7391.67	1705.77	42.644	93700	7808.33	1801.92	45.048
88800	7400.00	1707.69	42.692	93800	7816.67	1803.85	45.096
88900	7408.33	1709.62	42.740	93900	7825.00	1805.77	45.144
89000	7416.67	1711.54	42.788	94000	7833.33	1807.69	45.192
89100	7425.00	1713.46	42.837	94100	7841.67	1809.62	45.240
89200	7433.33	1715.38	42.885	94200	7850.00	1811.54	45.288
89300	7441.67	1717.31	42.933	94300	7858.33	1813.46	45.337
89400	7450.00	1719.23	42.981	94400	7866.67	1815.38	45.385
89500	7458.33	1721.15	43.029	94500	7875.00	1817.31	45.433
89600	7466.67	1723.08	43.077	94600	7883.33	1819.23	45.481
89700	7475.00	1725.00	43.125	94700	7891.67	1821.15	45.529
89800	7483.33	1726.92	43.173	94800	7900.00	1823.08	45.577
89900	7491.67	1728.85	43.221	94900	7908.33	1825.00	45.625
90000	7500.00	1730.77	43.269	95000	7916.67	1826.92	45.673
90100	7508.33	1732.69	43.317	95100	7925.00	1828.85	45.721
90200	7516.67	1734.62	43.365	95200	7933.33	1830.77	45.769
90300	7525.00	1736.54	43.413	95300	7941.67	1832.69	45.817
90400	7533.33	1738.46	43.462	95400	7950.00	1834.62	45.865
90500	7541.67	1740.38	43.510	95500	7958.33	1836.54	45.913
90600	7550.00	1742.31	43.558	95600	7966.67	1838.46	45.962
90700	7558.33	1744.23	43.606	95700	7975.00	1840.38	46.010
90800	7566.67	1746.15	43.654	95800	7983.33	1842.31	46.058
90900	7575.00	1748.08	43.702	95900	7991.67	1844.23	46.106
91000	7583.33	1750.00	43.750	96000	8000.00	1846.15	46.154
91100	7591.67	1751.92	43.798	96100	8008.33	1848.08	46.202
91200	7600.00	1753.85	43.846	96200	8016.67	1850.00	46.250
91300	7608.33	1755.77	43.894	96300	8025.00	1851.92	46.298
91400	7616.67	1757.69	43.942	96400	8033.33	1853.85	46.346
91500	7625.00	1759.62	43.990	96500	8041.67	1855.77	46.394
91600	7633.33	1761.54	44.038	96600	8050.00	1857.69	46.442
91700	7641.67	1763.46	44.087	96700	8058.33	1859.62	46.490
91800	7650.00	1765.38	44.135	96800	8066.67	1861.54	46.538
91900	7658.33	1767.31	44.183	96900	8075.00	1863.46	46.587

Salary Conversion Table

Annually	Monthly	Weekly	Hourly	Annually	Monthly	Weekly	Hourly
97000	8083.33	1865.38	46.635	102000	8500.00	1961.54	49.038
97100	8091.67	1867.31	46.683	102100	8508.33	1963.46	49.087
97200	8100.00	1869.23	46.731	102200	8516.67	1965.38	49.135
97300	8108.33	1871.15	46.779	102300	8525.00	1967.31	49.183
97400	8116.67	1873.08	46.827	102400	8533.33	1969.23	49.231
97500	8125.00	1875.00	46.875	102500	8541.67	1971.15	49.279
97600	8133.33	1876.92	46.923	102600	8550.00	1973.08	49.327
97700	8141.67	1878.85	46.971	102700	8558.33	1975.00	49.375
97800	8150.00	1880.77	47.019	102800	8566.67	1976.92	49.423
97900	8158.33	1882.69	47.067	102900	8575.00	1978.85	49.471
98000	8166.67	1884.62	47.115	103000	8583.33	1980.77	49.519
98100	8175.00	1886.54	47.163	103100	8591.67	1982.69	49.567
98200	8183.33	1888.46	47.212	103200	8600.00	1984.62	49.615
98300	8191.67	1890.38	47.260	103300	8608.33	1986.54	49.663
98400	8200.00	1892.31	47.308	103400	8616.67	1988.46	49.712
98500	8208.33	1894.23	47.356	103500	8625.00	1990.38	49.760
98600	8216.67	1896.15	47.404	103600	8633.33	1992.31	49.808
98700	8225.00	1898.08	47.452	103700	8641.67	1994.23	49.856
98800	8233.33	1900.00	47.500	103800	8650.00	1996.15	49.904
98900	8241.67	1901.92	47.548	103900	8658.33	1998.08	49.952
99000	8250.00	1903.85	47.596	104000	8666.67	2000.00	50.000
99100	8258.33	1905.77	47.644	104100	8675.00	2001.92	50.048
99200	8266.67	1907.69	47.692	104200	8683.33	2003.85	50.096
99300	8275.00	1909.62	47.740	104300	8691.67	2005.77	50.144
99400	8283.33	1911.54	47.788	104400	8700.00	2007.69	50.192
99500	8291.67	1913.46	47.837	104500	8708.33	2009.62	50.240
99600	8300.00	1915.38	47.885	104600	8716.67	2011.54	50.288
99700	8308.33	1917.31	47.933	104700	8725.00	2013.46	50.337
99800	8316.67	1919.23	47.981	104800	8733.33	2015.38	50.385
99900	8325.00	1921.15	48.029	104900	8741.67	2017.31	50.433
100000	8333.33	1923.08	48.077	105000	8750.00	2019.23	50.481
100100	8341.67	1925.00	48.125	105100	8758.33	2021.15	50.529
100200	8350.00	1926.92	48.173	105200	8766.67	2023.08	50.577
100300	8358.33	1928.85	48.221	105300	8775.00	2025.00	50.625
100400	8366.67	1930.77	48.269	105400	8783.33	2026.92	50.673
100500	8375.00	1932.69	48.317	105500	8791.67	2028.85	50.721
100600	8383.33	1934.62	48.365	105600	8800.00	2030.77	50.769
100700	8391.67	1936.54	48.413	105700	8808.33	2032.69	50.817
100800	8400.00	1938.46	48.462	105800	8816.67	2034.62	50.865
100900	8408.33	1940.38	48.510	105900	8825.00	2036.54	50.913
101000	8416.67	1942.31	48.558	106000	8833.33	2038.46	50.962
101100	8425.00	1944.23	48.606	106100	8841.67	2040.38	51.010
101200	8433.33	1946.15	48.654	106200	8850.00	2042.31	51.058
101300	8441.67	1948.08	48.702	106300	8858.33	2044.23	51.106
101400	8450.00	1950.00	48.750	106400	8866.67	2046.15	51.154
101500	8458.33	1951.92	48.798	106500	8875.00	2048.08	51.202
101600	8466.67	1953.85	48.846	106600	8883.33	2050.00	51.250
101700	8475.00	1955.77	48.894	106700	8891.67	2051.92	51.298
101800	8483.33	1957.69	48.942	106800	8900.00	2053.85	51.346
101900	8491.67	1959.62	48.990	106900	8908.33	2055.77	51.394

SPECIAL MEETING OF THE BOARD OF DIRECTORS OF

(NAME OF CHURCH)

A meeting of the Board of Directors was held on _____, 20____, at the offices of the Church located in _____ at _____ p.m. Waiver of Notice and Call of the Meeting was presented by the Secretary and filed in the Church corporate minutes.

Board Members Present:

Guest Present: (if applicable)

There being a quorum present the President and Chairman of the Board called the meeting to order:

The Chairman of the Board of Directors asked the Secretary of the Corporation to read the minutes from the previous meeting.

Motion: Motion made by _____ to accept the minutes as read.

Seconded: _____ seconded the motion.

Passed Unanimously.

*   *   *   *   *

New Business:

The Chairman and President brought to the attention of the Board of Directors that it was appropriate for the Board to consider the compensation level for Pastor _____ for the calendar year 20___, and to validate the amounts of reasonable compensation for all highly compensated Church employees. In such regard, the Chairman indicated that, in preparation for a review of Pastor's compensation package, advice of counsel was requested regarding the laws and limitations of reasonable compensation, and regarding the consequences to the Church of any increase in the pastor's salary or fringe benefits.

The Church's counsel gave a report to the Board on the subject of reasonable compensation. Counsel reminded the Board that, for churches, excessive compensation or unreasonable compensation will result in inurement with the possible consequence of revocation of tax-exempt status. Mabee Petroleum Corp. v. U.S., 203 F.2d 872 (5th Cir. 1953); Founding Church of Scientology v. U.S.,

412 F.2d 1197 (Ct. Cl. 1969); People of God Community v. Comm'r., 75 T.C. 127 (1980).

However, counsel also indicated to the Board that the "reasonableness" standard for compensation is the same for nonprofit and for-profit organizations. Enterprise Ry. Equipment Co. v. U.S., 161 F. Supp. 593 (Ct. Cl. 1958).

Generally, according to counsel's report, many factors are relevant in determining whether compensation is reasonable, and no single factor is decisive; the totality of facts and circumstances must be weighed. Foos v. Comm'r, T.C. Memo. 1981-61.

The Tax Court in the Foos case crafted the most commonly cited reasonable compensation variables:

- Employee's qualifications and training;

- Nature, extent, and scope of duties;

- Responsibilities and hours involved;

- Size and complexity of the business;

- Results of the employee's efforts;

- Prevailing rates for comparable employees in comparable business;

- Scarcity of other qualified employees;

- Ratio of compensation to gross and net income (before salaries and federal income tax, if appropriate of the business;)

- Salary policy of the employees;

- Amount of compensation paid to the employer to its other employee in prior years;

- Employee's responsibility for employer's inception and/or success;

- Time of year the compensation was determined;

- Whether compensation was set by corporate directors;

- Correlation between the stockholder-employee's compensation and his stockholding;

- Corporate divided history;

- Contingent compensation formulas agreed on prior to the rendition of services and based upon a free bargain between employer and employee;

- Under-compensation in prior years;

- Compensation paid in accordance with a plan which has been consistently followed;

- Prevailing economic conditions;

- Whether payments were meant as an inducement to remain with the employer; and

- Examination of the company after payment of compensation.

Later, in the Elliotts case according to the Church's counsel, the Ninth Circuit Court of Appeals functionally divided all reasonable compensation factors (the Foos 21 factors plus others developed through litigation) into five broad categories:

1. Employee's role in the company.

2. External Comparison - comparison of employee's salary with those paid by similar companies for similar services.

3. Character and Condition of the Company - size, as indicated by sales, net income or capital value, and the complexities of the business and general economic conditions.

4. Conflict of Interest - (1) Whether some relationship exists between the company and its employee which might permit the company to disguise nondeductible corporate distributions of income as salary expenditures deductible under 162 (a) (1) - (2). Existence of free bargaining in determining compensation and the perspective of hypothetical independent investor in evaluating the compensation payments. (Elliotts) case indicates that a potentially exploitable relationship may exist whenever the employee is in the company's sole or controlling shareholder - may give rise to rebuttable presumption that compensation was set without the benefit of arm's length bargaining.

5. Internal Consistency - Overall company treatment of payments to employees - Evidence of inconsistency may indicate that payments go beyond reasonable compensation - Existence of long-standing, consistently applied compensation plan is evidence that questioned salary payments are reasonable.

Counsel briefed the Board on the perceived attitude of the IRS regarding reasonable compensation for churches, pastors and church employees. According to counsel, it is clear that the IRS believes that the jobs of many nonprofit executives and other positions cannot be compared accurately to compensation for similar services performed for other for-profit organizations because comparable data is not available. Counsel suggested that the clergy undoubtedly fell in this category, and counsel was sharply critical of this attitude of the IRS, and indicated that data was more available today enabling a pastor's job description to be compared favorably with many for-profit positions, including that of the chief executive of a small, closely held corporation.

Further, counsel brought to the attention of the Board that, from counsel's knowledge and experience, IRS examining agents have stated frequently that any salary exceeding $100 thousand in an exempt organization setting will be cause for alarm, and if not properly documented, may result in a more extensive examination of an organization already undergoing an audit. Counsel indicated that there was absolutely no basis for such a standard, and that from knowledge and experience he was aware of many salaries in excess of $100 thousand in church and ministry settings which, in his opinion, were supported under the circumstances.

Finally, counsel informed the Board that a certain attitude continues to prevail at the IRS that persons called to church service and careers in the clergy

were seen by the IRS to accept a substantial compromise from their alternative ability to earn reasonable for-profit executive compensation even if the for-profit job description is virtually identical to the nonprofit job description. Counsel was harsh in his comments about this so-called "vow of poverty" syndrome that is widespread at the IRS, and elsewhere, but which is extremely prejudicial to the rights of clergy. Counsel suggested that such attitude and other perceptions-related problems unfairly keep the clergy at below-market, unreasonably low compensation levels, but that such conclusions were meritless, and slowly are becoming disregarded in court and in compensation law.

Counsel briefed the Board on the core issue of how presumptively to establish reasonable compensation for the Church; the issue of prudent compensation setting and implementing methodology for a church whose pastor receives compensation and, with his family or close associates, controls the board. A detailed discussion focused on the problem of inurement in this setting, where the potential for abuse appears to be so serious that the IRS requires evidence of arm's length bargaining between the pastor receiving compensation and the board of the church establishing the compensation. Counsel indicated to the Board that it is incumbent upon the Board to insulate itself from being the exclusive compensation determining and implementing body, and that reliance upon outside expert assistance was required in order to protect the Church and the members of the Board.

Counsel reminded the Board that, absent some carefully conceived method of establishing reasonable compensation for the Church's highest paid employees, the IRS easily could disagree and find the Board's determination to constitute excess compensation, resulting in inurement to an insider, and forming the basis of a possible revocation of the Church's tax-exempt status.

At this time, it was counsel's recommendation that the Board consider an effective solution to this problem without having to appoint a number of outside Directors (effectively relinquishing control of the Board) in order to establish arm's length bargaining between the inside Board and the pastor or other highly-paid employees. It was suggested by counsel that a reputable, qualified consulting firm be commissioned by the Board to review the compensation structure of the Church in order to prepare a study, or evaluate and make recommendations to the Board for the purpose of establishing and implementing reasonable and proper compensation for the Church

Counsel indicated that proposals could be obtained from reputable clergy compensation consulting groups for this type of work, but that in the event that the cost of such an evaluation or study was beyond the resources of the Church, an acceptable reputable outside counsel (unaffiliated with the Church), stating that established compensation was reasonable, and that the implementation of such reasonable compensation by the Board on behalf of the Church insiders. Counsel informed the Board that several reputable law firms have established credibility for compensation work, enabling such counsel to provide "reasonable compensation" opinions which are defensible before the IRS, and which provide to church boards of directors inurement insulation comparable to the alternative of a comprehensive compensation study.

In summary, counsel indicated to the Board that either of the suggested methods will enable the Church to demonstrate a prudent approach to the determination of reasonable compensation, and that the real value of such an investment, in addition to the satisfaction the Church and pastor receive from payment of proper and reasonable compensation, is to enable the Church to settle quickly any compensation disputes the Church or pastor ever have with the IRS.

Other factors cited in support of obtaining a study or compensation opinion of counsel include:

- Increase likelihood that adjustments would be made in lieu of litigation if compensation is the only audit issue.

- Protection (insurance) against revocation of exempt status based upon inurement.

- IRS will respect study/opinion approach with impressive work-product by reputable consulting firm or law firm.

- Strong defensibility of study findings provides excellent basis for Board compensation decisions.

- Comfort to Church inside counsel who might otherwise be required to give legal opinions for reasonable compensation levels, but who is not entirely disinterested.

- Although study may be expensive, investment is a wise expenditure compared to cost of protected defense of a proposed revocation proceeding by IRS arising from compensation set by inside board without reliance upon outside professionals and experts.

- May be only safe alternative to under compensation.

- Compare cost and utility of before-the-fact compensation planning "testimony" with after-the-fact study, experts or planning - issue of prudence and credibility.

The Board considered the report of counsel through extensive discussion. Generally, the Board concluded that the future of the Church's compensation structure was an area requiring outside help, and was a sensitive and dynamic area. It was also determined that in order to establish proper and essential loyalty to the Church from its most important employees, the engagement of a consulting firm or outside counsel in order to validate clergy and church compensation would have a positive impact upon the Church's employees' self-esteem and sense of value to the Church. The expense would be an investment in morale.

The President indicated that a Motion would be appropriate regarding the report and recommendations of counsel, and solicited a Motion from the members of the Board.

Motion made by _____ to investigate the use of a qualified church and clergy compensation consulting firm, or a reputable law firm experienced in church compensation matters, for the purpose of validating amounts of reasonable and proper compensation for the Church's highest paid employees.

Seconded: _____ seconded the motion.

RESOLVED: That the Board of Directors of the Church direct the Church's officers to solicit bids and proposals from qualified consulting firms and/or outside legal counsel, to propose to the Church a study, analysis, evaluation, opinion or comparable method of determining and validating reasonable and proper compensation for the Church and its employees.

RESOLVED: That the officers of the church commit their time and church's resources, to the extent reasonable and necessary, in order to obtain proposals for this work for the review and consideration of the entire Board of Directors of the church.

Passed unanimously.

* * * * *

Continuing New Business:

The president indicated that, even after resolving as a Board to begin the process of reviewing the Church's compensation structure, it was appropriate to consider whether an immediate adjustment, on the cost-of-living and/or merit basis, to the Pastor's salary was appropriate. In this regard, the President indicated that he had asked the Church's counsel to review the circumstances of the Church's recent performance under the Pastor, and the Pastor's salary for the previous two years. Counsel present a brief report on this subject.

Counsel indicated that in preparation for the report to the Board there was extensive coordination with_____, the Church's external bookkeeper, IRS information return preparer, and financial consultant. The results of such coordination have enabled counsel to present a written report on the Church's financial performance over the two year period. The written report, prepared by _____, was distributed to the Board members present at the meeting.

The conclusion of the financial report is that the Church has prospered financially under the leadership of the Board of Directors, and of the Pastor.

This was discussed as a factor influencing the amount of any merit compensation raise to be considered for the pastor. Additionally, the _____ firm recently conducted a comprehensive project to review clergy compensation, including analyzing Bureau of Labor statistical information, with a two-year analysis of the U.S. consumer price index. Counsel informed the Board that, through a coordinated effort with _____, counsel has concluded that a modest _____ raise for the Church's Pastor is justifiable. Counsel recommended that the amount of such adjustment be ___% of the _____ salary, but recommended generally that any adjustment between ____% and ____% is supportable.

The recommendation of counsel, and the financial report prepared by _____, were reviewed and discussed extensively by the Board.

After discussion, the President suggested that a Motion may be in order, and solicited a Motion from the Directors present.

Motion made by _____ to award to the Church's Pastor a combined merit/cost-of-living raise for the calendar year _____ (retroactive to _____) in the percentage amount of ___% _____ salary. Said amount equates to $_____ annually.

Seconded: _____ seconded the motion.

The Motion was put in the form of a resolution:

RESOLVED: That the Board of Directors, on behalf of the Church, increase the Church Pastor's salary, retroactive to January 1, _____, in

the annual amount of $ _____, which amount equates to____% of the Pastor's _____ salary.

RESOLVED: That the officers of the Church take any and all measures and actions deemed appropriate and necessary to the implementation of such salary adjustment, including proper written communication to the Pastor, Church Payroll and bookkeeping/internal accounting departments, and to _____ in order to ensure that the Church's financial and nonprofit compliance requirements are met.

Passed Unanimously.

The President asked for additional business; there being no additional business, the meeting was adjourned with prayer.

Secretary _____

Date _____

Date approved for entry

_____

(Seal)

Pastor's Employment Contract

This **Employment Contract** is entered into this _____ day of _____, 20____, between the ("**Church**"), a _____ corporation, and (State)
Pastor _____ ("**Last Name**").

Whereas, _____ is an experienced pastor, having pastored churches other than the **Church** and is qualified to serve as the pastor of the **Church**; and

Whereas, Church is in need of a pastor to lead the **Church** spiritually, scripturally, morally and to oversee the administration, business matters and day-to-day activities of the **Church**; and

Whereas, the congregation, membership, management and leadership of the **Church** has duly considered the application of _____ to serve as the pastor of the **Church**; and

Whereas, _____ immediately and substantially can contribute to the success of the **Church**, in its spiritual, financial, physical and secular needs; and

Whereas, _____ **has demonstrated to the satisfaction of the Church** his desire to lead the **Church** as its pastor, his qualifications to serve as pastor, and his calling to be pastor of the **Church**; and

Whereas, Church and _____ decide to enter into a contract for the employment of _____ as the pastor of the **Church** on the terms and conditions herein set forth:

Now therefore, Church and _____ hereby agree as follows:

1. **Employment. Church** does employ _____ as its Pastor-President for a period of _____ years, which shall begin on the execution hereof and which shall end on the first day of _____, 20___.

2. **Compensation.** In payment for his services as Pastor, **Church** shall pay to _____ a base annual compensation of _____ Thousand Dollars ($_____) for each twelve (12) month period thereof, which shall be payable in equal installments on the 1st and 15th day of each calendar month during such period. In addition to _____'s base annual compensation, **Church** shall provide _____ with a parsonage in kind or, alternatively, a housing rental allowance in compliance with Section 107 of the Internal Revenue Code. In the event that **Church** provides a parsonage in kind, the parsonage shall be equipped and furnished in a dignified manner and to the reasonable satisfaction of_____ _____ so that _____ and his family shall be able to maintain a standard of living comparable to the needs and requirements of the Pastor of the **Church**. In the event a Code Section 107 Housing Allowance is provided to _____, same shall be sufficient to accommodate _____'s actual housing expenses necessary to maintain a personal residence with a fair market value in the range of $150-200 thousand. In no circumstances shall any such housing allowance exceed the actual expenses associated with payment for, maintenance of furnishings, utilities, upkeep and the reasonable expenses associated with such housing. Additionally, in no circumstance shall the annual total of any such housing allowance exceed one-half (50%) of _____'s actual annual base compensation

payment for any twelve (12) month period.

_____ additionally shall be eligible to participate in all retirement plans, tax deferred annuities, tax sheltered annuities, tuition remission/salary deduction or other forms of prerequisites or retirement benefits which are or become available from time-to-time for any employee of the **Church**. To the extent _____ incurs any expense associated with his duties and responsibilities as Pastor of **Church**, same will be eligible for reasonable reimbursement pursuant to **Church's Accountable Reimbursement Plan** as filed with the offices of the Secretary of the **Church**. _____ shall be provided with term life insurance in an amount not to exceed _____ hundred thousand dollars ($_____) during the term of the **Employment Contract**, the premiums for which shall not exceed $ _____ per annum in the aggregate. **Church** shall pay reasonable health insurance costs incurred by _____, not to exceed Five Hundred and no/Dollars ($500.00) per month.

3.   **Duties of Pastor.**

A.   _____ shall serve as the Pastor-President of the **Church**, subject at all times to the ultimate control and direction of the Board of Directors of **Church**. It is hereby expressly understood, agreed and provided that _____ shall perform and discharge such other and/or further duties as may be assigned to him from time-to-time by the Board of Directors of the **Church**.

B.   _____ agrees that during and throughout the term of the **Employment Contract**, he will devote such of his time and energies as may be required in order for him to carry out, fulfill and perform the

duties and responsibilities to be performed by him under the terms of this **Employment Contract.**

C. _____ shall not become involved in any business matters which may adversely affect the **Church** or the performance of his duties and obligations under this **Employment Contract**.

D. The **Church** finds its headship under the Lord Jesus Christ and in its Pastor. The Pastor-President shall be the Chief Executive Officer of the **Church**. He shall be a continuing member of the Board of Directors throughout the term of the **Employment Contract.** The Pastor-President shall have general management of the business of the **Church** and general supervision of the other officers. The Pastor-President shall preside at all meetings of the Board of Directors and shall see that all orders and Resolutions of the Board are carried into effect; subject, however, to the right of the Board to delegate to any other officer or officers of the **Church** any specific powers, other than those that may be conferred upon the Pastor-President. The Pastor-President shall execute in the name of the **Church** all deeds, bonds, mortgages, contracts, and other documents authorized by the Board of Directors. The Pastor-President shall be ex-officio a member of all standing committees, and shall have the general powers and duties of supervision and management usually vested in the office of president of a corporation. No person shall be invited to speak, teach or minister at a meeting held by the **Church** without the Pastor-President's approval. He shall be designated attorney-in-fact for the **Church** by virtue of his office. The Pastor-President shall have the authority to appoint and approve any assistance that would be reasonable necessary to carry on the work of the Lord properly.

4. **Non-Competitive Covenant.**

A. During the term of this **Employment Contract** and for a period of

two (2) years from and after the date of _____'s termination of employment with the **Church**, if _____ voluntarily terminates his employment, and one (1) year from and after the date of _____'s termination, if _____'s employment is involuntarily terminated (hereinafter referred to as the "Non-Compete Period"), _____ shall not engage or provide services, as an employee or on a self-employed basis within a one hundred (100) mile radius of _____ (City), _____ (State), or a one hundred (100) mile radius of the site of worship services regularly conducted at the **Church** ("Non-Compete Area"), as pastor, principal, agent, associate pastor, or in any other capacity with another church, or in any similar business which would compete with the membership, loyalty, direction, religion, philosophy or activities of **Church**, or become a principal, owner, leader, director, or employee of any church-related business, ministry, religious association or other organization which may attract, compete for or have any interest in the congregation, membership, finances, donor-base or business activities of **Church**.

Further, during such period, _____ will not, directly or indirectly (through immediate family members or otherwise), support, recommend, assist, own, manage, finance, operate, control, participate in, be employed by or be connected in any other manner with any such activity within the Non-Compete Area in competition with, pursuit of or similar to the membership, activities and business affairs of the **Church**. During such period,_____ _____ further agrees that he will not, either directly or indirectly, through any person, firm, association or corporation with which he is now or may hereafter become associated, cause, induce or encourage any present or future member, congregation, officer, employee or leader of **Church** or any of its affiliates to leave the employee, membership or association of **Church** or any such affiliate to accept employment with _____ or with any

such person, firm, association or corporation, or with any business that conducts a business within the Non-Compete Area in competition with or similar to or directly related or ancillary to the activities, business affairs and related matters of the **Church.**

The foregoing agreement not to compete between _____ and the **Church** shall not be held invalid or unenforceable because of the scope or territory or actions subject thereto or restricted thereby, or the period of time within which such agreement is operative; but any judgment of a court of competent jurisdiction may define the maximum territory and actions subject to and restricted by this paragraph 4, in the period of time during which such covenant is enforceable.

B.   All provision hereof for the protection of the **Church** are intended to be for its benefit and enforceable directly by the **Church.** _____ _____ agrees that any remedy at law or for any violation of the terms hereof would be inadequate, and that the **Church** shall be entitled to specific performance hereof or injuctive relief, or both, by temporary remedy, writ or order as may be entered by a court of competent jurisdiction, in addition to damages that the **Church** may be legally entitled to recover or other remedies which the **Church** may be legally to avail itself of, together with reasonable expenses of litigation, including attorneys' fees incurred in connection therewith, as may be approved by such court, and _____ further agrees to waive any requirement for the securing or posting of any bond in connection with the obtaining of any such injuctive or equitable relief.

5.   **Miscellaneous Provisions.**

A.   **Enforceability; Waiver.** In case any term, phrase, clause, paragraph, restriction, covenant or agreement contained in this paragraph shall be

held to be invalid or unenforceable, the same shall be deemed, and it is hereby agreed that the same are meant to be several, and any such invalidity or unenforceability shall not defeat or impair the remaining provisions hereof. A waiver by the **Church** of any breach of this contract by_____ _____ of any duties imposed upon_____ hereunder or by law shall not be construed as a waiver by the **Church** of its rights hereunder for any subsequent or continuing breach of this contract of any of the duties, obligations or agreements herein contained or imposed by law.

B. **Binding Effect**. The provisions of this contract shall be binding upon and inure to the benefit of the parties hereto, their personal legal representatives, heirs, successors and assigns.

6. **Termination**. The term of this contract shall be as set forth in paragraph 1 hereof, (i) unless _____ shall sooner die, whereupon this contract shall terminate, or (ii) unless this contract shall be sooner terminated by _____ as herein provided for, or (iii) unless the **Church** shall terminate this contract as provided for in the next successive paragraph hereof. In the event this contract is so terminated,_____ _____ shall have the right to compensation as set forth in paragraph 2 hereof, to the end of the month in which the termination becomes effective, but not otherwise.

_____ may, at any time, by giving **Church** six (6) months prior written notice, terminate this contract for any reason whatsoever. If at any time after the Commencement Date the **Church** commits a material breach of the terms and provisions of this contract and fails to cure such breach prior to the expiration of ten (10) days after the delivery by _____ to the **Church** of written notice setting forth the nature and extent of such

breach, _____ may terminate this contract thereafter by prompt written notice of such termination delivered to the **Church**, which form of termination shall render void and unenforceable any non-competitive covenant or related provision of paragraph 4.A. and 4.B. hereof. The failure by _____ to exercise his right to terminate this contract with respect to any one or more of the matters referred to in this paragraph 5.A. shall not be taken or held to be a waiver by _____ of his right to terminate his contract in respect of that breach (provided it shall be continuing) or of any subsequent breach.

     A.   The **Church** may, at any time subsequent to twelve (12) months after the Commencement Date, without cause, by giving _____ ten (10) days prior written notice, terminate this contract by paying_____ _____the sum of _____ Thousand Dollars ($_____), or the **Church** may terminate this contract for any one or more of the following reasons:

      (i)   If _____ shall be found pursuant to the **Church** due process proceeding to have engaged in any unscriptural, fraudulent, dishonest or deceitful activities, including without limitation, the following:

          (a)   adultery;

          (b)   embezzlement;

          (c)   conviction of a felony; or

          (d)   any other act which may be deemed a violation of federal, state or local law (except misdemeanor or traffic offenses).

      (ii)   If _____ shall become ill or become injured or

otherwise become so incapacitated that he cannot, in the reasonable good faith opinion of the Board of Directors of the **Church**, carry out fully and perform his duties hereunder, and such incapacity shall continue for a period of four (4) months, the **Church** may, when such incapacity persists, give to _____ written notice of such termination, and this contract shall be terminated ten (10) days thereafter. In such circumstances the **Non-Competitive Covenant** provisions to paragraph 4.A. and 4.B. hereunder may be waived at the discretion of the **Church** Board of Directors.

(iii)   Notwithstanding any provision to the contrary hereunder with respect to _____'s resignation, removal or termination, any such termination shall be pursuant to the due process described in the By-Laws of the **Church**.

In the event _____ should choose to leave voluntarily, he shall designate his successor. Said designated successor shall be chosen with the advice and consent of the Board of Directors, the Board of Advisors and the Board of Elders if such Boards exist.

In the event that the pastor shall have serious charges as described in this contract brought against him, the matter shall be brought before the Board of Elders, if such Board exists. If the Board of Elders is not active, the matter shall be brought before the Board of Directors. In the event the matter cannot be resolved at a meeting of the Board of Elders, power is then vested in the Board of Directors, the Board of Advisors and the Board of Elders collectively to come together with the Pastor to consider his removal. Upon rec-

ommendation of removal, a two-thirds (2/3) majority vote of the members of the congregation present at a meeting duly called for such purpose shall be required for removal. The associate pastor or some other person designated by the Board of Advisors, Board of Elders or Board of Directors, shall represent the combined Board of Directors, Board of Advisors and Board of Elders and chair the meeting of the members of the congregation.

The order of business at such meeting of the members of the congregation shall be as follows:

(a)   roll call;

(b)   presentation of evidence by the combined Board of Directors, Board of Advisors and Board of Elders;

(c)   presentation of case by Pastor or his designee;

(d)   rebuttal evidence presented by combined board;

(e)   testimony from members of the congregation for vote.

Upon a conclusion of **Church** due process that the Pastor should be removed, the terms and provisions of removal, termination and due compensation as described in the contract shall be applicable.

B.   The failure by the **Church** to exercise its right to remove _____ or terminate _____'s employment under this contract with respect to any one or more of the matters referred to in paragraph B above or with respect to any incapacity of _____ which would give rise to the **Church** having a right to terminate this contract, as provided for above, shall not be taken or held to be a waiver by the **Church** of its right of termination of this contract in respect of that breach or incapacity

(provided it shall be continuing) or of any subsequent breach or incapacity. Paragraph B shall not limit the **Church's** rights or remedies, other than in regard to termination, for a breach of this contract by_____.

7.   **Vacations**. _____, without reduction in compensation, shall be entitled to not less than two (2) weeks of vacation time during any fiscal year of the **Church**. **Church** and _____ agree that additional yearly vacation time can be arranged for _____ by mutual agreement, and upon the approval of the Board of Directors. Vacation need not be consecutive and may not be accumulated from year to year.

8.   **Prior Agreements**. Any and all prior agreements with respect to the employment of _____ by the **Church** are hereby revoked, and this **Employment Contract** is, and is intended by the parties to be, an integration of any and all prior agreements or understandings, oral or written, with respect to the employment of _____ by the **Church**.

In witness whereof, Church and _____ have set their hands the day and year first above written.

_____

Name of Church

By:_____

Chairman, Board of Directors

_____

Director

_____

Director

_____

Director

_____

Director

_____

(Pastor's Signature)

Employment Contract & Special Clauses

1. Clause to be placed in pastor's employment contract:

"In the event that all or any portion of the above mentioned compensation paid to Pastor_____ (or any officer/employee of the church) is determined by the Internal Revenue Service and upheld by a court of competent jurisdiction to be excessive compensation on the grounds that it is not reasonable, posing a threat that such excess payment may result in inurement benefiting a private person, the recipient of such excessive payment agrees to reimburse the church to the extent of the amount of such compensation found to be excessive within thirty (30) days after the church has notified him of such excessive amount. In this regard, the church, by and through its Board of Trustees, is hereby authorized by the pastor/officer to reach a settlement on this issue with the Internal Revenue Service, which settlement shall cause this provision to be enforced. In the event that the church reaches a settlement with the Internal Revenue Service as to the amount of reasonable compensation paid or payable, such settlement shall be conclusive and irrefutable evidence that any amount paid to the pastor/officer beyond such amount was excessive, and same shall be reimbursed to the church within said 30 day period or the church shall have the right to withhold up to 50% of any future compensation payments due to the pastor/officer until the amount owed the church pursuant to this provision has been paid in full." [Such a reimbursement clause could provide that the church must take the reasonable compensation issue to some specific stage of negotiation with the IRS, or in court, such as the Tax Court, before any reimbursement obligation arises. However, because excess compensation likely would be coupled with a claim of inurement threatening the tax

exemption of the church and possibly only one of some or many other items arising from a church audit, the safest form of latitude to the church would be to give the church the right to negotiate reasonable compensation with the IRS prior to commencing litigation.]

2. Statement of Understanding made by church pastor or other highly compensated officer.

"I certify that I am familiar with [identify the church's Board of Trustees' Resolution or Bylaw provision relating to excess compensation] requiring reimbursement of compensation payments made to me in my capacity as the pastor/officer of the church which are challenged by the Internal Revenue Service successfully as excessive for federal tax-exemption reasonable compensation purposes to the entire extent of such excessive amounts. Upon consideration of the mutual promises of the Board of Trustees and officers of the church, I agree to and declare myself bound by the terms of said [Resolution or Bylaw]."

3. Bylaw requirement.

"Any payments made to an officer or the pastor of the church, such as salary, housing , bonus, expense reimbursement or other, which shall be challenged in whole or in part by the Internal Revenue Service as excessive, or which may pose a threat to the tax-exemption of the church through inurement, shall be reimbursed by such officer or by the pastor of the church to the full extent of such excess. It shall be the duty of the Trustees, as the Board of Trustees, to enforce payment of each amount deemed to be excessive. In lieu of payment by the officer or pastor of the

church, subject to the determination of the Trustees, proportionate amounts may be withheld from future compensation payments to affected officers or the pastor until the amount owed to the church has been recovered in full."

There is strong authority respecting the propriety of excess compensation reimbursement provisions. Obviously, the examples arise under for-profit law under Code Section 162. The IRS has acquiesced in <u>Oswald v. Commissioner</u>, 49 T.C. 645 (1968), acq., 1968-2 C.B. 2. To meet the requirements of these authorities, it is necessary that:

1. Either a corporate bylaw or resolution of the Board of Trustees must require repayment of compensation found to be excessive or unreasonable;

2. The bylaw or resolution must be adopted prior to the year in which the compensation deemed to be excessive is paid;

3. The employee must enter into a signed agreement to repay the excessive amount of the bylaw or resolution prior to the year in which the excessive compensation is received; and

4. The agreement signed by the bylaw or resolution should be enforceable under state law.

The Executive of God

Dear Pastor,

In putting together "The Executive of God," Mr. Chitwood, and the staff of Chitwood & Chitwood, have condensed important information we feel is most essential in helping the Pastor plan for his financial well-being. In addition, we have endeavored to create an approach to this subject that is both enlightening and useful.

Our firm is dedicated to the Pastor and his well-being, and the subject of retirement planning is one which Mr. Chitwood feels is of special importance for the Pastor.

The Pastor does not receive the comprehensive benefit packages that key employees of private corporations take for granted. In addition, the Pastor often elects out of social security, leaving him without any type of assistance in preparing for his future.

Our firm believes the Pastor is the most important executive, "The Executive of God," and we are here to help the Pastor plan and provide for his future financial well-being.

Sincerely,

As most of you are already aware, our firm, Chitwood & Chitwood, is dedicated entirely to taking care of the Pastor. Our Philosophy is that those who hear the call and choose to follow that call should not be neglected. The Pastor is an "Executive of God." The Pastor is a well-trained, well-educated professional and deserves the same type of executive benefit package as any "Key Employee" in the private sector.

The ministry also has special needs. The ministry must preserve and protect its tax-exempt status and abide by the special provisions of the code which are directed toward nonprofit organizations. It must provide for its employees in a manner that will enhance and never endanger its status. Yet, it must provide. Being an organization which is exempted from tax under section 501(c)(3) of the code means that the entity was not established to make a profit. It does not mean that those who are key to the survival of the organization should have a substandard living.

A tax-exempt organization faces special problems. It cannot have shareholders or stock incentive programs. It cannot take advantage of a reorganization or qualify its property for special use valuation in the event of a family run ministry. It is imperative that those who are employed by a tax-exempt organization make use of every advantage the law allows.

Our firm believes that good stewardship is something that can be developed over time. You begin in a small way, with something as simple as remembering to make a notation each time you write a check, and with little help, your record keeping becomes accurate and you become aware of where you can best direct your resources. Sound financial planning need not be painful. In fact, you should soon realize an increase in your overall financial picture. Habits develop over time as we establish repetitive patterns for doing things. Once we learn to change from old routines to new ones, the situation around us will change effortlessly. We walk before we run and we begin by learning and gathering information.

On the following pages we will present an overview of programs which are available to serve the Pastor in his need for comfortable retirement, while enhancing his present financial situation through increased benefits and tax savings.

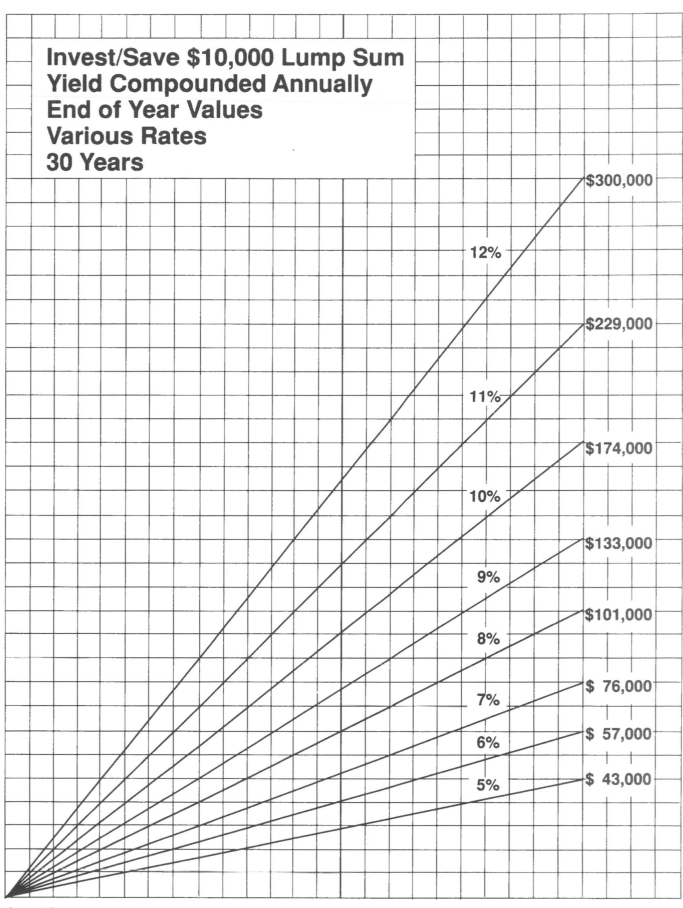

Invest/Save $10,000 Lump Sum
Yield Compounded Annually
End of Year Values
Various Rates
30 Years

$300,000

12%

$229,000

11%

$174,000

10%

$133,000

9%

$101,000

8%

$ 76,000

7%

$ 57,000

6%

$ 43,000

5%

Age 35

Age 65

107

Financial Statement - Balance Sheet

Name_____Date_____

Current Assets

_____ $_____
_____ $_____
_____ $_____
_____ $_____
_____ $_____
_____ $_____
_____ $_____
_____ $_____

Total $_____

Current Liabilities

_____ $_____
_____ $_____
_____ $_____
_____ $_____
_____ $_____
_____ $_____
_____ $_____
_____ $_____

Total $_____

Long Term Assets

_____ $_____
_____ $_____
_____ $_____
_____ $_____
_____ $_____
_____ $_____
_____ $_____

Total $_____

Long Term Liabilities

_____ $_____
_____ $_____
_____ $_____
_____ $_____
_____ $_____
_____ $_____
_____ $_____

Total $_____

Deferred Assets

_____ $_____
_____ $_____
_____ $_____
_____ $_____
_____ $_____
_____ $_____

Total $_____

Asset Grand Total $_____

Liability Grand Total $_____

Assets $ _____

Liabilities (_____)

Net Worth $_____

Ministry Sponsored Program for the Pastor

As the "Key Employee of a ministry or church, the Pastor's need for standard benefits to be provided is now being recognized. The Pastor has often opted out of Social Security, is raising a family, and has no retirement plan. The Church or Ministry will find it beneficial to relieve the Pastor of his future economic worries, especially if the ministry will have 0% total net outlay at the Pastor's retirement.

The Pastor and Ministry enter into an agreement which is drafted into a properly executed document. The document will specify an appropriate retirement age and income.

The Ministry then makes contributions into an investment vehicle which has several investment options, offers interest and growth on the funds, and assures that this interest is not currently taxable.

The investment vehicle may have a life insurance benefit, which allows the plan to be surrounded by favorable laws. If so, then the Ministry may pick and choose whom to include in the plan. This is not a pension plan for the entire organization, but a "Private Pension" for its key employees. The Ministry can later recoup its investment or provide an enhanced benefit to the Pastor. Either way, there is no longer an excuse for the Pastor to be without a salary continuation or retirement plan.

We feel this is an excellent benefit for the Pastor. It can continue the Pastor's income at retirement, or supplement what the Pastor will be receiving from other plans. It will not burden the Ministry with undue paperwork and <u>it will not place a financial burden on the Pastor.</u>

This will allow the Pastor to accumulate a retirement fund without placing a strain on his current financial position.

Tax-Sheltered Accounts (403(B) Plans)

A tax-sheltered account (hereafter referred to as 'TSA') offers immediate tax reduction, tax-deferred savings and generous contribution limits. Contributions are made with pre-tax dollars and are tax-deferred until received, as are the earnings on the contributions.

As a general rule, contributions should not exceed 16 2/3% of "Includable Compensation" but not to exceed $9,500 annually. Before making a contribution into a TSA Plan, an employee must enter into a salary reduction agreement with the employer.

This does not mean the employee earns less money, but that the employee would like to receive the money at a later date, and avoid paying taxes on it now. The employee decides how much to defer and that amount is credited to the employee's account. The money is invested and grows tax-deferred, as it would in an IRA. This means that the interest and is not taxed, providing a substantial accumulation of funds. Once the employee is ready to receive distributions, the amount of money accumulated is substantially more than what would be available in a taxable C.D.!

These plans are known as "Salary Reduction" plans, and although that may not sound appealing, it is the almost painless way to put aside money for retirement.

Let's say you earn $100 a week (for purposes of simplification). You decide you want to defer 7% of your paycheck

into the plan. You would deduct $7.00 from your pay, leaving income tax only on the $93.00. This reduces your taxable income by $28.00 a month and that $28.00 is invested and growing in your retirement account. In addition, the ministry might opt to match your contributions!

If you are a qualified tax-exempt organization under 501(c)(3) of the IRS code, you are eligible to set up a tax-sheltered account for your organization. (Section 403(B) of the code allows employees of tax-exempt organizations to defer a portion of their earnings from income taxes.)

TSA or 403(B) Plans are available only to chartered 501(c)(3) organizations. They require some paperwork to set up initially and then are simple to administer. The TSA or 403(B) Plan is a wonderful employee benefit which can be made available to all Ministry employees. It can offer help in saving for retirement on a before-tax basis. This plan will also permit an employee to contribute a larger tax deductible contribution than they could with an IRA.

How Much Tax Can I Save?

By participating in a TSA, you can realize a substantial tax savings, depending upon your tax bracket as well as the amount of your contributions.

Current Tax Savings

Tax Bracket	$1,200 Contribution	$2,500 Contribution	$5,000 Contribution	$9,500 Contribution
15%	$180	$375	$750	$1,425
28%	$336	$700	$1,400	$2,660
33%	$396	$825	$1,650	$3,135

Individual Retirement Account (IRA)

In addition to a ministry sponsored retirement program and a TSA, you can make additional tax deductible contributions into an IRA or Individual Retirement Account. Contributions must take into account any TSA contributions so as to not exceed the annual limit. As opposed to TSA Plans, an IRA is not "Deferred" from salary but is "Deducted" from earned income already received. The deductible contribution then earns interest on a tax-deferred basis.

Money which is invested so that it will grow tax-deferred is the fastest way to accumulate a substantial amount of money. The sooner you start to invest, the greater the rate of return. That is what is meant by the "Time Value Of Money..."

The following page contrasts two investors. Investor A opens an IRA and makes a $2,000 contribution at age 19 and each year thereafter, ceasing contributions at age 26.

Investor B waits until he is 27 to begin making contributions and continues to make contributions through age 65. Both projections assume a 10% rate of return. At age 65, Investor A has invested $16,000 and has a total of $1,035,160. Investor B has invested $78,000 and has an account value of $883,185. This is a particularly clear example of the Time Value of Money.

	Investor A			Investor B	
Age	IRA Contribution	Year-End Value	Age	IRA Contribution	Year-End Value
19	$2,000	$2,200	19	0	0
20	2,000	4,620	20	0	0
21	2,000	7,282	21	0	0
22	2,000	10,210	22	0	0
23	2,000	13,431	23	0	0
24	2,000	16,974	24	0	0
25	2,000	20,872	25	0	0
26	2,000	25,159	26	0	0
27	0	27,675	27	$2,000	2,200
28	0	30,442	28	2,000	4,620
29	0	33,487	29	2,000	7,282
30	0	36,835	30	2,000	10,210
31	0	40,519	31	2,000	13,431
32	0	44,571	32	2,000	16,974
33	0	49,028	33	2,000	20,872
34	0	53,930	34	2,000	25,159
35	0	59,323	35	2,000	29,875
36	0	65,256	36	2,000	35,062
37	0	71,781	37	2,000	40,769
38	0	78,960	38	2,000	47,045
39	0	86,856	39	2,000	53,950
40	0	95,541	40	2,000	61,545
41	0	105,095	41	2,000	69,899
42	0	115,605	42	2,000	79,089
43	0	127,165	43	2,000	89,198
44	0	139,882	44	2,000	100,318
45	0	153,870	45	2,000	112,550
46	0	169,257	46	2,000	126,005
47	0	186,183	47	2,000	140,805
48	0	204,801	48	2,000	157,086
49	0	225,281	49	2,000	174,995
50	0	247,809	50	2,000	194,694
51	0	272,590	51	2,000	216,364
52	0	299,849	52	2,000	240,200
53	0	329,834	53	2,000	266,420
54	0	362,817	54	2,000	295,262
55	0	399,099	55	2,000	326,988
56	0	439,009	56	2,000	361,887
57	0	482,910	57	2,000	400,276
58	0	531,201	58	2,000	442,503
59	0	584,321	59	2,000	488,953
60	0	642,753	60	2,000	540,049
61	0	707,028	61	2,000	596,254
62	0	777,731	62	2,000	658,079
63	0	855,505	63	2,000	726,087
64	0	941,054	64	2,000	800,896
65	0	1,035,160	65	2,000	883,185

Less Total Invested	(16,000)	**Less Total Invested**	(78,000)
Net Earnings:	1,019,160	**Net Earnings:**	805,185
Money Grew:	64-Fold	**Money Grew:**	11-Fold

115

An IRA is an individual plan which will allow you to deduct up to $2,000 from your taxable income. In addition, you do not pay taxes on the interest earned until withdrawn. This fulfills two purposes: 1) It lowers the tax you pay by allowing you to deduct your contribution when you file your income tax return; 2) It provides a "Shelter" for your money. The funds in your account earn "Interest on the Interest".

Recent legislation has added some new restrictions to IRA's. If you or your spouse is a participant in a qualified retirement plan you may lose some or all of your IRA's deductibility.

An IRA is something you should give serious consideration to if you are not eligible to participate in another qualified plan (employer plan, TSA, etc.). However, if you have another type of plan you might consider making a contribution into that plan instead. For example, in a TSA you contribute dollars before they are taxed; in an IRA you make the contribution and then take the deduction on your tax return.

Charitable Remainder Unitrust

Making a guaranteed charitable gift to your Ministry can increase your income, and lower your income, estate <u>and</u> gift tax liability! How? Through a Charitable Remainder Unitrust. Do you have an appreciated asset or a cash property donation you would like your ministry to ultimately receive, but you are concerned that your family might need money as well? By setting up a unitrust you can solve both problems.

The trust is established to receive the assets and is irrevocable. You designate a non-charitable beneficiary, such as your spouse, to receive an income for a certain number of years. You receive an income, estate and gift tax deduction for the actuarial value of the remainder interest. The tax deduction improves your rate of return on your investment plus lowers your ultimate estate tax liability. Your spouse or designated beneficiary receives an income stream and your ministry or charity is guaranteed the remainder. Life insurance may be considered in this type of trust to enhance your gift.

The Charitable Remainder Unitrust is a technique worth considering for anyone wishing to make a substantial contribution to a charitable beneficiary. The following chart will illustrate how the Unitrust can enable a donor to make a sizable contribution to a favorite charity, while retaining an income interest in the gifted money and property

How the Unitrust Works

*Yr.	Age	Contribution to Trust	Tax Deduction	Tax Savings	Out-of-Pocket Contribution	Unitrust Value
1	50	$30,000	$4,120	$1,153	$28,847	$33,000
2	51	30,000	4,608	1,290	28,710	69,300
3	52	30,000	4,967	1,390	28,610	109,200
5	54	30,000	5,774	1,616	28,384	201,400
7	56	30,000	6,717	1,880	28,120	313,000
9	58	30,000	7,896	2,211	27,789	448,100
11	60	30,000	9,349	2,617	27,383	611,500
13	62	30,000	11,159	3,124	26,876	776,200
15	64	30,000	13,439	3,762	26,238	1,008,500
17	66	0	0	0	0	1,055,400
19	68	0	0	0	0	1,104,500
21	70	0	0	0	0	1,155,900
23	72	0	0	0	0	1,209,700
25	74	0	0	0	0	1,266,000
27	76	0	0	0	0	1,324,900
29	78	0	0	0	0	1,386,600
31	80	0	0	0	0	1,451,100

| | Total Out-of-Pocket Contributions $412,883 | | Total Income Received $1,481,692 | | Total Contribution Charity $1,451,141 | |

Assuming a 28% income tax bracket, a 10% rate of return and a 7% annual pay-out.

118

The Lord tells us in 3 John 1:3 that "He wants us to prosper and be in health, even as our soul prospers." God wants us to fare well spiritually, socially, mentally, physically and financially - in that order. Just because you're a Christian doesn't mean you have to be poor. One of the ways a Christian glorifies God is by achieving financial success.

H. Michael Chitwood
Financial Counselor
"The Authority"

Worksheet for Retirement Needs

I plan to retire in how many years: .... _____

Currently Renting: .... _____
Own Home: .... _____

Monthly Rent: .... $_____
Mortgage Payment: .... $_____
Maintenance: .... $_____

Monthly Household Utilities: .... $_____
(Electricity, Water, Gas, Telephone, Cable TV)

Automobile Expense: .... $_____
(Payments, Insurance, Gas, Maintenance & Parking)

Clothing: (Expense per Person) .... $_____

Entertainment Expense (Monthly): .... $_____
(Movies, Dinners, etc.)

Travel Expense (Annual): .... $_____

Interest on Debt: .... $_____

School Tuition: .... $_____

Insurance Premiums
Life: .... $_____
Disability: .... $_____
Health: .... $_____
Homeowners: .... $_____
Business: .... $_____

Investments (Annual): .... $_____
Savings: .... $_____
Mutual Funds: .... $_____
Annual Retirement: .... $_____
Stocks & Bonds: .... $_____
Other: .... $_____

Total Annual Expenses: .... $_____

At what percent do you feel the cost
of living increases each year: .... _____%

Number of years to retirement: .... _____

Multiply number of years times cost of living percent
Multiply by annual expense amount .... _____

Current Salary: $_____

Expected Annual Increase: $_____

Years to Retirement: _____

Projected Salary at Retirement: $_____
(Expected Increase x Number of Years)

Expected Social Security Benefit: $_____
(Enter $0 if None)

Expected Housing Allowance at Retirement: $_____
(Enter $0 if None)

**Pension and Retirement Payouts
Available at Retirement:** $_____

**Total Dollar Benefits Available at
Retirement Minus Projected Salary =
Post Retirement Deficit:** $_____

Clergy, Tax & Law
Salary Survey

CTL welcomes your comments and suggestions to improve the scope and depth of the survey. Please assist us in this endeavor by completing the form below.

Are there any other positions that you would like to see included in next year's survey?

Job Title _____   No. in position _____

Job Title _____   No. in position _____

Job Title _____   No. in position _____

Please include your description for these jobs.

Title _____   Annual Salary _____

Title _____   Annual Salary _____

Title _____   Annual Salary _____

Title _____   Annual Salary _____

General comments and suggestions:

_____

_____

_____

_____

_____

Individual _____   Title _____

Organization _____

Address _____

City _____   State _____ Zip _____

Phone Number _____

Clergy, Tax & Law
1-800-345-9117

122